PRAISE FOR *SHE FLIES WITHOUT WINGS*

"A gem of a book . . . Midkiff takes us on a fascinating journey. . . . If you've had, or hoped for, the richness and challenge of a horse in your life, you'll enjoy this book. **Experience the magic.**" —*Horse & Rider Magazine*

"**Mary Midkiff should never ride faster than her Guardian Angel can fly—and apparently she hasn't, hence this delightful book.**"
—**Rita May Brown, author of** *Catch as Cat Can*

"**As Midkiff elegantly points out, horses are both substantial and tangible—they are big, powerful animals—and ethereal, representative of myth and magic for millennia. . . . A thoughtful exploration . . . that should appeal to women and girls who love horses, as well as those who dream of them.**"
—*The Daily Camera*

"*She Flies Without Wings* **goes beyond the physical relationship between females and horses to explore the deeper connection that binds a gender and a species.**"   —*Rocky Mountain News*

"**Part autobiography, part social and natural history, and part literary work . . . Horsewomen, or women who long to be horsewomen, will thoroughly enjoy this book.**"   —*Booklist*

"**Poignant . . . Her stories are honest—sometimes gritty, sometimes sweet—and always touching. . . . Midkiff truly understands what a woman's relationship is with her horse. . . . A compelling read and a spiritual uplift.**"   —*Horse Illustrated*

"**Midkiff explores the multiple dimensions in the relationship between a horse and rider . . . two athletes seeking the synchrony of a single mind and heart. This book is a perfect example of the relationships, meanings and values women take from and bring to sport—gifts of depth that all sportsmen and sportswomen should spend time exploring.**"
—**Donna Lopiano, Ph.D., executive director, Women's Sports Foundation**

SHE FLIES

WITHOUT

WINGS

How Horses Touch a Woman's Soul

Mary D. Midkiff

Illustrations by Nancy Denison

Delta
Trade Paperbacks

A Delta Book
Published by
Dell Publishing
Random House, Inc.
1540 Broadway
New York, New York 10036

ISBN: 0-385-33500-8

Reprinted by arrangement with Delacorte Press, a division of Random House, Inc.

Manufactured in the United States of America

Published simultaneously in Canada

March 2002

10 9 8 7 6
BVG

For Horse Angels
For the Rise of the Feminine Spirit

CONTENTS

When Allah created the horse, he said to the wind, "I will that a creature proceed from thee. Condense thyself." And the wind condensed itself, and the result was the horse.

Marguerite Henry, King of the Wind

INTRODUCTION

A woman's relationship with a horse is an encounter between the intangible—the spiritual, the mythical, the ethereal—and the *very* tangible: the physical, everyday realities of riding, horsekeeping, and life itself. In my life and in the lives of many women, the two extremes meet and merge seamlessly, contrasting and explaining each other in a way that makes both realities more clear. The concrete act of being outside on my horse, the gritty actuality of dust and dirt and wind and sun, somehow stirs the less shaped and more inexplicable interior within me. The tactile experience of brushing my mare gives me a sense of larger connectedness with my universe. A horse's body and limbs are not only palpable but symbolic, not just functional but suggestive. My mare—any horse—is more than merely the sum of her bodily parts; she is an embodiment and a model of power, grace, balance, and intuition. What's more, in a horse's natural business of foaling, raising young, integrating herself into horse society, handling risk and danger, living, aging, and dying, she is a demonstration of instinctive behaviors and attitudes that can find a healthy and helpful place in almost any woman's life.

Women and horses have always been drawn to one another. They rode together in Greek myth and Celtic poem, Native American legend and Wild West folktales. In Colonial Williamsburg in Virginia, the journals, bills of sale, and estate inventory lists of eighteenth-century ladies depict a feminine life that always included horses. There are references to dress, riding habits, carriages, saddles, and harness horses. One woman's account of her daily routine with her cart horse has been used as the basis for one of the historic site's colonial riding and driving presentations. At the National Sporting Library in Middleburg, Virginia, the rare-book vaults contain the advice of nineteenth-century schoolmasters that women should ride "gently" along with explanations of the "medical considerations" of a woman's riding. The correspondence of agricultural fair managers discloses that all-woman exhibitions of riding and racing were promoted as fund-raising attractions in the 1800s. In any suburban library today, the children's and young adult sections are literally stuffed with horse stories, most of them written for girls. In London entire bookstores are devoted to the literature of horses, and when I huddled for days among their stacks, most of my fellow shoppers were horsewomen like myself. Women and horses emerge in life and literature as a huge tribe of spiritual sisters.

It is probably no accident that women and horses are finding each other in unprecedented numbers as the new millennium opens. Twentieth-century Western women achieved an unparalleled freedom of choice in their work, play, movement, dress, and lifestyle. Twentieth-century horses underwent their own liberation, from the work-and-war role of history to an easier, recreational place in human lives. Social, religious, economic, and practical barriers that once limited interaction fell during the 1900s. Today girls and women represent more than 80 percent of the participants in all horse-related activities in the United States. A creature that lost its job of moving us across town and across country to the automobile and other vehicles carries us again. Only now our destinations are different. When I think back over my own life with horses and talk to women who share the same sense of connection, what emerges is that our relationships with horses are taking us to new levels of personal confidence and power, teaching us compassion and acceptance, showing us more natural ways to resolve problems in our daily lives.

She Flies Without Wings is a book extending our natural connection with horses into the sacred realm where we expand our understanding of ourselves and better our relationships with others. Because horses have made such a difference in my own life, I have used many of my own life experiences to frame this discussion. Other women have been generous and shared their experiences, too. To season all these "real" episodes, excerpts from Eastern and Western mythology, horse juvenilia, travel accounts, contemporary fiction, poetry, song, and essay are interwoven with the narrative. Legendary creatures cohabit on the pages of this book with goddesses, outlaw cowgirls, royalty, and modern women.

In choosing these excerpts, I've included only the selections I love best, an admittedly personal standard. Some came from tattered old storybooks that have been sitting on my own shelves since my girlhood. Others are souvenirs from an adventure in literary discovery I set out on when I started this book. This has been a journey that took me from the steppes of China to the shores of Iceland, from antiquity to yesterday. The tales of horsewomen such as Celia Fiennes and Isabella Bird, the outlaw Belle Starr and the trick rider Annie Oakley reminded me that horses have been powering women past stereotypes and gender boundaries for centuries. "Meeting" these women and others— the rough-around-the-edges ladies who drove cattle in the American West, the homesteaders who made a living from their land, the women warriors who fought on horseback, the European princess who felt at home only in the saddle—brought wonderful new kindred spirits into my life, just as my travels and horse clinics do. I know many men love horses, too, and I haven't slighted them. Geoffrey Chaucer didn't overlook horses in his tales, and William Shakespeare had so much to say about them that whole books are written about his equine pennings. There is perhaps no passage more etched into the equestrian world's literary tradition than the Prophet's words in the Koran.

> After God had fulfilled his word, he addressed the newly created mare as follows: "I have made thee without an equal: the goods of this world shall be placed between thy eyes; everywhere I will make thee happy and preferred above all the beasts of the field, for tenderness shall everywhere be in the heart of the master; good alike for the chase and retreat, thou shalt fly though wingless . . ."

BUT NOW IT is *our* turn to be heard about these magical creatures and how they move and teach us. As Sir Laurens van der Post put so aptly in his memoir about himself and his horse, Blady, "As far as the male was concerned, the horse was part of a masculine elitism and entertainment, but in the world of the feminine he was sought out for his own sake and for the pleasure and the lift of imagination he gave, particularly to young girls, so that by the time they were adolescent and about to move on into life, they had reached that new moment of birth into themselves helped by schooling and graduating from ponies up to horses."

The selections included here are not intended to be comprehensive or even representative of the literary tradition of the horse or the relationship between women and horses. I have intentionally steered away from the "dark" literature—the funerary and devil images, the tales of sexual deviance, sacrifice, and dismemberment. Sadly, few diaries recounting women's lives with their horses have survived, and most that do come from educated, well-to-do women who had the time and resources to keep journals. We probably will never know how the peasant women, whose hard lives often relied on horse labor, experienced these relationships. For the most part, I've included passages that shed light on the themes I have explored in my life and that I know other women want to explore: nurturance, transformation, danger, creativity, acceptance, and all the rest.

She Flies Without Wings is organized into twelve chapters that loosely mirror the arc of a woman's life—from our discovery as young girls of a natural affinity for the horse and our own sensuality, through the quest and development of qualities such as compassion and power, to an emerging awareness of life's changing seasons and a growing spirituality.

If there is a dominant theme, or one that emerges and

reemerges throughout, it is acceptance in its many incarnations. Horses constantly test the boundaries of acceptance between and among themselves, much as people do; in their own unique way, they set the standards of acceptance in their relationships with their human caregivers; and they naturally strive for contentment in their daily lives, a serenity achieved only through self-acceptance under a wide range of circumstances. In writing this book, I came to understand that acceptance of myself was and is my ultimate goal. Horses help show the way. They teach, give, and bring me freedom.

It is what I wish for us all.

A NATURAL AFFINITY

I grew up in New England: Massachusetts, Maine, and Rhode Island. I never rode as a child, although I had my own imaginary horse that I rode around my grandparents' backyard. I obsessively drew horses and wrote poems about them colliding in the sky with brilliant colors around them. Returning to this subject matter as an adult, and subsequently learning how to ride, is like reliving the adolescence I never had and fulfilling a dream deferred.

Patricia Cronin, "Pony Tales,"
from Horse People, Writers and Artists
on the Horses They Love

*W*hen I was six, I was a horse.

My home was in the heart of central Kentucky on just the sort of white-fenced Thoroughbred horse farm the words "bluegrass" and "Kentucky" suggest. My father managed the breeding farm and crop operations, which gave my family the right to live in the manager's house. While I slept in this house, I lived as much as possible in the barns and pastures where the rest of my herd grazed. That's how I thought of the mares and foals and weanlings and yearlings at Hartland Farm: as my herd.

If you had spied me with my herd, you would have seen a girl, small for her age, perched precariously atop the post-and-board fence that bordered the Hartland fields. You might have noticed legs too short to reach the second rail. You would not have known I was a horse and that I felt my legs were long and fluid as young saplings stirring in the wind. Even a foal learning how to use her legs can be elegant.

When I leaped off that rail and into the horses' pastures,

as I often did, I galloped with grace and purpose. I could run with the breezes, or stand still and feel them skim over my flesh. I could bounce out a rhythm or roll down a hill. I could swing my hair, and it would wave in my trot like a long, flowing tail. I learned all this—and more—from horses. I saw that when a horse moves across the open field, it's as if she's following the call of a voice in the air. Her head rises, her ears prick forward to receive a message in horse frequency, and her nostrils open to catch sensory signals drifting by. She doesn't use her tongue to respond; she pushes out feral answers from the hollow between her ribs. At times, all four of her great limbs leave the ground in a display of perfect suspension—one hoof coming down, followed by another and another and another until all have touched earth just long enough to renew the effortless cycle. She gains ground but without need for anything more than stirring the air and enjoying a good talk with her universe. When I moved in the way my herd moved, I felt in my legs the same balance and rhythm and coordination I saw in theirs and I strained toward the voices they heeded. I gained fluency in a body language my own small body was not born knowing but which it longed to speak. In the fields, I listened to the way the horses cleared their nostrils when grazing and called to each other in whispered rumbles of affection or squealed with joy or warning. This was the language of my herd, and I studied it as diligently as I studied my other language, the one of my family. I became good at whinnying, snorting, and delivering those sounds, and the horses learned my voice.

Occasionally they included me in their play. They would nibble at my ankles or rub their flanks against my own knobby knees. When I poked my head through the openings between the planks and extended my arm forward, curious foals came to smell my hand. After they got to know me and recognize my scent, they came even closer—nuzzling my head and trying to take a taste of my pigtails. I giggled at the feel of their busy lips on my head and their warm breath on my neck.

A horse's acceptance remains one of my earliest memories of belonging. While I struggled to find who I was and would be as a person, horses gave me my first intimation of what acceptance and belonging could feel like.

. . . .
This baby arrived amid a herd of horses,
*   horses of different colors.*

White horses ride in on the breath of the wind.
White horses from the east
where plants of golden chamisa shimmer in the
*   moonlight.*

She arrived amid a herd of horses.
Blue horses enter from the south
bringing the scent of prairie grasses
from the small hills outside.

. . . .
She arrived amid a herd of horses.

Black horses came from the north.
They are the lush summers of Montana and still white
*   winters of Idaho.*

Chamisa, Chamisa Bah. It is all this that you are.
You will grow: laughing, crying,
and we will celebrate each change you live.

You will grow strong like the horses of your past.
You will grow strong like the horses of your birth.

By Luci Tapahonso
Blue Horses Rush In
For Chamisa Bah Edmo, Shisóí 'aláají 'naaghígíí

WHEN I WAS a girl of six, I thought I was the only girl-horse in the land and the broodmares and offspring of Hartland my only herd. Now I know horses touch the souls of many women.

Horses are giant yet generous with their strength, their power, and their gentle affection. By their very nature, they embody and resolve the contradictions we all struggle with: They are strong and soft, calm and driven, wild and manageable, needy and independent. In the presence of horses, our impulses of nurturing and our urgent needs of support, strength, and confidence come together, live together, and express themselves together without the noise of intellectualism. We see that the horse lives its own life, speaks in its own way, moves where it needs to go. Its directness and simplicity offer a thousand-pound counterpoint to our own complicated and often less-honest human interactions. The horse shows us how to be complete.

When a woman first meets the horse, she feels fear and awe, respect and caution, excitement and reserve. She reaches out to stroke the horse's side and remembers the first touch of a lover's hand. The soothing warmth of connecting to another spirit with its own power and its own passion washes over her. She runs her fingers through the horse's mane and looks into his eyes, finding there a companion who says *Let's go places together. Everything is better with me.* As she strokes the velvet muzzle, he licks her fingers and softens his gaze, lowering his head and extending himself to her in a way that makes her heart swell and race at the same time.

Later she questions the encounter. She puzzles over the tangle of fear and inspiration—even euphoria—the moment brought her and wonders if she could have only imagined a connection with this great, elusive animal. From unfamiliar recesses of her being, new longings push into her consciousness. She imagines being lifted to the horse's back and carried to far-off places. She is tempted. She must see the horse again.

And she does. The next time she approaches with her hand held out in a tentative gesture of greeting, and he reciprocates by pointing his ears toward her and nosing at her fingers. He has smelled this hand before but he checks once again, just to be sure. She responds by stepping closer, running her hand up his nose and gently scratching between his eyes.

He lowers his head, blinks. He is saying *All right. I'll let you into my world.* She steps around to his side and moves his mane out of the way to stroke his neck. As it did the first time, the warmth of connection washes over her. She feels the definition of the muscular yet swanlike neck. He's enjoying this, too; she knows because he doesn't turn away.

She begins to think of the horse more personally. She notices the variety of colors in his coat hairs and how they sparkle in the sunlight, the texture of his mane and how the threads taper down his neck perfectly to shield him from the weather when he is still but lift and float to add symmetry to his shape when he begins to run. She sees fluff inside his ears and is surprised to discover that each ear swivels independently of the other but that both follow her body and her noises, as do those great liquid eyes, which track her every step. Even his breathing matches hers, speeding up and slowing down with her own.

In the horse, she glimpses a model for escaping everyday stress and releasing everyday pressures. She feels a sense of wellness she can take back into her hectic life. Her emotions stir, her instincts are fed, she draws nearer to her own sensual self. A horse's home environment gives the woman sanctuary where she can experience each moment of life in its singular perfection or imperfection. She believes the horse will lead her to a peaceful place within herself.

This is enough for now. It is enough for her to know the first encounter was not a dream. On her way home, she decides she could never live life without revisiting and reinvesting these insights. It is as if her life started when she met the horse. Before that it was all just practice.

The Hullocks [hills] were blackening as Velvet cantered down the chalk road to the village. She ran on her own slender legs, making horse-noises and chirrups and occasionally striking her thigh with a switch, holding at the same time something very small before her as she ran. The light on the chalk road was the last thing to gleam and die. The flints slipped and flashed under her feet. Her cotton dress and her cottony hair blew out, and her lips were parted for breath in a sweet metallic smile. She had the look of a sapling-Dante as she ran through the darkness downhill.

Enid Bagnold, *National Velvet*

MY GRANDFATHER WAS a hardboot horseman, a phrase typically applied to a Kentucky horseman who dealt only in hard cash and hard whiskey. (It apparently derives from an old-time, relatively derogatory characterization of a groom or other farmhand from the Bluegrass, who could be identified by his rawhide boots, which due to their lack of finish would turn very hard when they dried out after being wet.) He owned, trained, bred, insured, and lived horses from the early 1900s until he died, on my birthday, in 1990, and he was the only member of my family who came close to understanding my affinity for horses. To my father, horses were for work; to my mother, they were simply larger versions of the rabbits and moles and baby birds I insisted on keeping. But my grandfather understood the horse as a force that could sweep a soul to the top of the world. Like me, he saw everything that moved as the shadow image of a horse. Even when he drove his car and pulled out to pass another vehicle, he snapped his fingers and pumped the steering wheel as if he were heading for the finish line. He was race-riding a horse at full gallop. When I was in the car with him, I *was* a horse at full speed.

Though he was the only other horse person in my family and he took me to the races and pushed our car past others until I felt the thunder of racing hooves beneath me, my grandfather was of the old school that believed the horse world was no place for a lady. I remember a morning when he took me with him to breakfast at the racetrack kitchen, where all the horse people gathered every day. I was ten years old, and I was proud to hold his hand when we entered the cafeteria line. Everyone said hello to "Mr. Dan," who was PaPa (which came out "paw-paw") to me. As the jockeys and trainers asked about his horses and traded horse stories, I listened intently, fascinated by this backstretch world.

Once we were seated and eating our eggs, I asked PaPa if I could ride one of the lead ponies used to exercise the racehorses. He said, "No, I don't think there's one we can borrow this morning." I persisted—"Isn't there anything I could ride, or at least pet in your barn?"—but he continued to put me off with an impatient "We'll see."

After breakfast we drove to his training barn and I met his assistant and grooms. I drank in the smell of the place—the liniment, the steam coming off the just-bathed horses, the white quilted saddle pads hanging out to dry. It was intoxicating. When my grandfather finished with his business matters, I returned to the subject of riding or petting or merely getting close to one of the horses. Grudgingly he agreed I could put a hand on one of the lead ponies if I was very careful.

I was happy to touch one, but touching seemed a meager crumb compared to the feast I might have enjoyed. On our way home, I couldn't resist bringing up the ride I didn't get. "PaPa," I said, "there were lots of lead ponies out there. After the morning work, they stood around without anything to do all day. Couldn't you find one for me to ride?" I'd finally struck a nerve. He'd gone as far as he could; he could not bring himself to go any further.

His hands tightened on the steering wheel and he turned a stern face to me. "Mary Dike," he said, using the double name almost no Southern girl is without, "the racetrack is no place for a lady. You better get off your high horse and start thinking about doing something else when you grow up, like working in a restaurant or a beauty salon."

To my PaPa, I was only a girl. He was happy to lead me into the pasture and even let me stretch a hand through the rails to touch a velvet nose. But he believed the fields belonged to the boys. If I wanted to run with the real horses, I had to go find them on my own. And I did. There were other gates to other pastures. I sought them alone.

My work today brings me into close contact with thousands

of women every year. I recognize the heart of a horsewoman whenever I see a:

- Taste for the natural world
- Willingness to get dirty and to sweat
- Wish to experience a sense of power
- Longing to explore new spiritual frontiers
- Desire to be transformed
- Hungry soul

Just a little while ago, when I needed to go out to race a bit and throw my head in the wind, she stopped me, my dam-mother, and asked me who I thought I was. A girl? A horse? My name? I know what she's thinking. The others at school ask me the same question.

So I said, A girl, because I know that's what I'm supposed to think. One thing I know, not a girlygirl, which would be stupid playing games talking teasing being tied to the junglegym. I won't. That sometimes I'm a girl, sometimes I'm a horse. When there are girl-things to do, like read, which a horse never does, or go in the car to the stockshow or for ice cream or any of those things, I have to be a girl, but when there are hillsides of grass and forests with lowhanging boughs and secret stables in loquat trees, I am a horse.

Catherine Petroski, *"Beautiful My Mane in the Wind"*

MY FAMILY LEFT Hartland when I was nine. The farm was sold and the new owner brought in her own team of managers. We left the rolling fields of the bluegrass and all of my animal friends for a three-bedroom house on a main street in Lexington, Kentucky. I was bereaved and angry; for months I tried not to speak to my parents. I was a horse sealed within the world of people. I needed to find a new herd.

I found it two blocks away, in the big house behind the smaller one where my grandparents lived. The Daltons were one of the wealthier families in town, and their home was a fantasy world of space and toys and possibilities. Among these was a vast attic stuffed with antique vanity dressers full of old clothing and furs and jewelry and a family that included two daughters who, like me, were horses. Dee, a year younger than I, was a hot-blooded and temperamental horse, competitive and capable of violence. Allie, two years younger than Dee, was a quiet pony. Our kinship as horses became apparent as we searched for common ground the way all young children do. When I told them about Hartland, their yearning to canter through the fields and roll in the grass and whinny and snort didn't require words for me to recognize. I had seen it in the foals and the yearlings and felt it in my heart and limbs.

I met other girls when I moved to Lexington, but only in Dee and Allie did I find girl-horses like myself. The spacious Dalton house and yard became my new Hartland and Dee and Allie my new herd. Our girlhood games were many and varied but overwhelmingly horsy. In the attic, we rummaged the dressers and trunks looking for costumes and accessories to use in our portrayals of good and bad horse owners. Often we moved our operation out of doors—into the big backyard—where we would rope ourselves together into a team of fine harness horses or where one of us would play the trainer, working another on a long line. We held races and shows to display our prowess to our parents, siblings, and anyone else who would watch.

I had always spent a good deal of time moving around on all fours, but now I perfected the skill until I became startlingly good at it. I won most of the races we staged in the deep summer grass, and, later, when we added low jumps and then higher jumps, I often won those, too. On occasion, other girls would ask to join us and we would let them, but we knew they weren't horses and secretly we laughed because their jumps looked silly and awkward while ours were controlled and graceful. We trained hard and, on race or show days, wove streamers and ribbons into our manes. Sometimes we transported our shows to my own small yard nearby so my parents could watch. I remember them laughing and clapping at our stunts. Other people might have thought we were strange, but my parents only shrugged. *I guess she's just a horse*, they would say.

> *I used to walk in my sleep. On clear nights when the seals barked and played in phosphorescent waves, I climbed out the window and slept in a horse stall. Those "wild-child" stories never seemed odd to me; I had the idea that I was one of them, refusing to talk, sleeping only on the floor.*
>
> Gretel Ehrlich, *The Solace of Open Spaces*

LIKE MANY GIRLS, I begged for a horse all my childhood, and, like many girls, I came from a family without the means to buy and support my dream. Once, when we still lived at Hartland Farm, in an uncharacteristic display of generosity, my PaPa stepped in and paid fifty dollars to the Pink Pony Farm—a local seduction complete with Pepto-Bismol—colored fences—to buy me a black-and-white Shetland pony named Ginger. Since feed and board were free to us at Hartland, the pony was a bargain. I was thrilled when Ginger arrived with the green Western saddle and red bridle that were part of the deal. He couldn't have been more adorable than he was that day, standing still, tied to a post.

Unfortunately, standing still while tied to a post was about the only time he was adorable. Ginger was incorrigibly bad-tempered. My little-girl skills of horse handling didn't begin to match his capacity for damage. I could ride only within a tiny enclosed pen or with someone leading us; beyond those contained situations, even my father couldn't control him. As painful as it was to discover and admit, a pony I couldn't ride or play with was little better than no pony at all. In the end, Ginger was more decoration than friend. When we left Hartland, Ginger stayed behind and I went back to horsy games and fantasies supplemented by riding lessons and whatever other moments I could steal on the backs of other people's horses.

Five years later, my father tried to help. He found a nice Tennessee Walking Horse mare that—like Ginger—we could afford, especially now that I was old enough to work and pay for her feed and upkeep. Dad hoped Blue would silence my pleadings. She did, but not because my horse dreams had come true. The total financial and physical responsibility for this large and significant animal was a dose of reality I wasn't quite ready to swallow. What's more, I began to grasp that I didn't long to own just *any* horse; I longed to own a horse that could lift me to heights my own legs could not. Blue deserved a sedate owner who would pamper and protect her, and that wasn't me. It wasn't fun riding or leading the mare around in circles in a ring, all by myself, week after week. She was a nice mare with her nice walking-horse pace, but she didn't excite me. We weren't going anywhere together, and I was unexpectedly lonely. I was a gregarious young girl, and riding alone didn't feed my social pull. In the few months we owned Blue, I developed my first inkling that I needed a herd that included horses and people alike, not merely Blue and a deserted arena. We ended up finding the mare a home with family friends and I went back to dreaming.

It has been a long time since I was a girl-horse. I am a woman now. I have found a woman's ways of satisfying my yearnings for grace and rhythm and freedom and the power to soar over fence rails. But my ways still include horses, and I continue to learn from the herd. My current horse, Theodora, is my mare and my Muse. She cleanses me spiritually, physically, and intellectually. Most days I work for several hours in my office, then head for the stable where Theo lives. On the way, I stop at the market and pick up apples and carrots for my friend. The drive to the farm takes fifteen minutes. When I arrive, I step into Theo's world.

Usually she is welcoming. She pricks her ears to funnel my calls and responds by looking for me in the distance. As I near her, her face softens and she drops her head to my level. I give her a carrot or two, place the halter over her head, and lead her to the gate. As we move, I stroke her neck and talk to her. Her eyes fill with contentment, her ears flop with comfort. There is no need to renew our friendship and catch up; we are old, best friends who pick up wherever it was we left off. At other times when she hears my call, she does not turn to greet me. She has days when she prefers to remain in her horsy world rather than join me in mine. These moods are far and few between, but I empathize with them and take them into account. On days such as this, I might replace our workout under saddle with some mentally stimulating ground exercises or simply take her out on the trail rather than work on competitive techniques.

Often Theo is sunbathing in her pasture when I reach her. Before I snap the halter and ask her to stand up, I take a moment to enjoy the horse's closeness to the ground. Standing, she is a stretch for me at over sixteen hands; for this moment, we are equals who see eye to eye. After a lifetime around horses, I am still moved whenever I approach and greet a reclining horse and see no evidence of the natural instinct of fear and flight. A feral horse would never be caught lying down. Because they live on a precipice of real and imagined dangers, horses are always ready to run or defend themselves. Even their sleep is a defensive doze in which their eyes flicker open periodically and their ears remain cocked. Theo's faith in me as she lazes close to the earth gives me this moment of wonder. Sometimes I pause to join her there, spooning my back into the curve of her long elegant neck, closing my eyes, and supporting my head with her mane line, at peace within the embrace of our bond.

MADELYN AND HER MUSTANG
(A CLASSROOM ESSAY)

The neon red numbers flashed 1–0–0. Butterflies swirled in my stomach. To think that I would be getting a horse! Any horse I wanted. Any color, any size, any shape. I turned away from the clock and fell asleep to the rhythmic shadow of the neon lights reflecting on my wall.

I woke up an hour later, hoping for the big 3–0–0 flashing, the hour when we would leave for the mustang sale. It was only 2–0–0. I watched each minute pulse away until they finally totaled 3–0–0. I leapt out of bed, jumped into my clothes, and ran out the door straight into our gray Suburban. Before I knew it, the motor was running and the sweet temptation of sleep was held out right in front of me. My eyelids, try as I might to stop them, gently closed and I fell into a deep slumber.

When I woke up we were almost there. A thin crisp layer of snow covered the ground. I read the rectangular green sign on our left—Cañon City. We turned onto a long road. To our right was a prison. The large blue sign in bold letters read—

B.L.M.
Bureau of Land Management

We headed down a long dirt road, pulled into a parking lot, and waited. Blue vans drove up with patrol officers in them, and we were instructed to get in. We all shuffled in and were driven down toward cornfields. We turned a corner and headed downhill.

Then there it was: a huge field filled with wild mustangs in pens; all the colors made it look like an oil painting blotched with deep browns and reds. Earthy tones covered the fields in every color of a horse a girl could dream of having. We coasted down the hill and the vans pulled up in front of a small, old white building with green trim that was chipping off. I climbed out of the car and the sweet and musty scent of horses came to my nose. A tall, gaunt man with a fiery red mustache came out of the building to greet us.

"Hi, my name is Fran," he said in a rough cowboy way. The crowd timidly murmured their hellos back. Fran led us down to the horses. We had the choice of mares, stallions, or foals. My family and I chose mares, for I had always wanted a girl horse.

Fran took us to a huge corral full of horses. Their eyes were wide and full of fright, clouds of mist blew out their soft muzzles. Their long winter coats were frosted with ice. At each brisk movement someone made, the horses ran, the whites of their eyes showed and tails were tossed high, flinging up chunks of mud and snow. They flinched at all the loud sounds. Every horse ran but two: two bay mares, one a light plump horse with no winter coat, the other cute and fuzzy with a tint of brown in her black mane. They would not run, but instead lifted their heads to see from where the movement came.

I selected the plump bay mare. My parents had their eyes on the cute fuzzy one. We discussed this for some

*time. I overheard a girl and a man discussing which
horse they wanted. Before I could do anything, the plump
bay mare was being loaded into a red, four-horse trailer.
The girl and man drove away with the prize mare, taken
right out from under my nose. I sighed a deep cloud of
steam. I leaned up against the chipped metal fence as my
toes went numb from the cold. I looked at the little fuzzy
mare. Her brown eyes were full of intelligence. She was
young enough for us, I thought, and she was cute.*

*Around midday I came to a decision. I liked the bay
fuzzy mare. She might even be pregnant. A filly, I
thought. Then I would have it all! I announced my decision to my parents. We talked with Fran in the little white
building about how much it would cost. I left them and
went to look at my mare one more time. Her brown fur
was thawing out. It was then I noticed the pretty little
star on her forehead that had been covered up earlier by
a thick brown forelock. Yes, I thought, she is the one.*

Madelyn Sullivan, at age thirteen (1995)
Frisco, Colorado

SENSUALITY

Come to the stable. Come to where the horses are, and the sweet grainy, pungent smells. A horse has the headiest, most satisfying scent of all animals. Mostly because of what he eats. . . . A horse's breath is a mixture of warm apples and chicken soup. Everything to do with horses, their food, tack, bedding, smells very good. Everything feels good, the leather, a silky handful of oats, the cool metal of a bit, and the smooth licked edge of the manger.

Monica Dickens, Talking of Horses

*W*omen ride and long to ride horses for many reasons. We ride to find excitement and danger and power and freedom. We ride to explore the outside world and the one inside ourselves. We ride as a form of expression and communion and escape.

We ride to enjoy their bodies.

The horse's domain is a physical one, and it calls upon us to be physical. Riding requires us to understand and guide with our thighs, our weight, and our posture. Astride a horse, we stop thinking about our too-big hips or our too-small breasts—all those real and imagined flaws we women are so good at finding in ourselves. Mounted, we think only of how our bodies can best work with our glorious partner's.

Horses invoke our senses. Our houses and workplaces are structured, sanitized settings. The places where horses live and carry us are not. In our homes and at our jobs, our ears are filled with thrumming motors, clicking keyboards, beeping cash registers. On a trail, no matter how close to the city it lies, we are soothed by the timeless rhythm of hooves falling on bare earth.

When we ride, we sweat, and our sweat purifies us, forcing out the toxins and tensions trapped under our skin. The moisture from our pores snakes from the edge of our hairlines and down our spines. We smell our own heat. We are alive and mobilized in the muscles that cross our backs and run the length of our legs, along our calves, and to our toes. As young girls, many of us were warned against enjoying our bodies. Not so long ago, we were told that sensuality in a woman was unseemly, unladylike, unacceptable, even risky. Even though physicality in women has become more acceptable in recent years, many of us have never fully shaken off those early restraints. For us, riding is one of those rare approved venues where our senses are liberated and where we enjoy the rewards of that liberation. After all, riding requires us to become aware of our bodies and activate all those senses that little else in our lives calls upon. Sigmund Freud hypothesized and fantasized about the sexual aspect of women and horses. Women who ride or who seek the company of horses don't need Freud to explain the connection. Horses transport us across the borders of prohibition and inhibition and carry us into our sensual selves.

I grew up in Woodford and Fayette counties in central Kentucky, always convinced that straw, the limey dust of calcium oxide, and horse sweat smelled sweet and familiar—comfortable somehow. At Hartland, my playhouse during the daytime hours when the mares and foals were in the pastures was the hayloft of the horses' barn. I spent countless hours there in a sensory haze: My skin itched from the dry straw that littered its floors; my ears filled with the coos of pigeons that roosted in its rafters and the tick-tick-tick of tiny mouse paws scurrying across the planks; my nose opened to the clean, grassy scent of droppings. Even the ammonia that drifted up from the stall floors held a hint of perfume.

The highlight of my hours in the barn came at suppertime, when the horses were led in for the night. From outside, the mumbles of grooms snapping lead ropes to the mares reached my ears. Then, in a single-file line, the mares and foals entered the barn aisle, their hooves striking the hard concrete floor in a rhythmic one-two, one-two, one-two pulse that muted only when they reached the stalls filled with fluffed-up layers of crunchy golden straw. Between the rough slats of the loft's floor, I could study the wide back of a mare far beneath me and imagine myself gliding through space upon her. My knees scraped across the floorboards as I crawled to the edge of the opening where hay was thrown down and into her hayrack. Lying on my stomach, I hung my head over the edge of the hole fourteen feet above the ground until I made myself giddy with the height and the headiness of the mare's air and space. Suspended high overhead, it was easy to imagine the mare and I flying without wings.

As it does for most of us, the sensual side of life unfolded for me over a long period of time and, for the most part, in private. The discovery of physical pleasure—whether it was dangling my head through the floor of a loft at six or the stirring of sexual awareness some years later—was far too personal and unsettling for me to talk about. Yet it was never my secret alone. More often than not, my discoveries were bound up in my life with horses. Horses were triggers for my childhood senses, sensors of my adolescent hormones, partners in my mature adult body awareness. They remain to this day my gateway to the physical world.

> *[Belle Starr] was a beautiful sight as she rode away through the fields; her lithe figure clad in a closely fitting jacket, erect as an arrow, her hair unconfined by her broad-brimmed, feather-decked sombrero, falling free and flung to the breeze, and her right hand plying the whip at almost every leap of her fiery steed.*
>
> Samuel W. Harman, *Hell on the Border*

AT FIFTEEN, I took my first paying job—as a groom and stable hand at the small family farm where I took riding lessons. It was demanding, physical work whose chief attraction was not the amount of money it paid, which was paltry, but the entry I gained to the pastures and barns and paddocks where horses lived and where I might gain some hoped-for free riding time.

It was an awkward time of life—a time of sweaty palms, oily hair, pimples, and braces on my teeth. At school, the boys' voices were beginning to break, their Adam's apples to bulge, and their faces to fuzz over. We were all at an awkward age, but we were beginning to notice one another all the same. Just as weanlings and yearlings do when their hormones kick into gear, we watched and waited and occasionally took a graceless run at each other, testing the sensation of pairing up within the herd. In the barn, I felt none of the awkwardness I did at school. My palms didn't sweat, and my hair, skin, and braces didn't matter. The horses didn't care what I looked like or how I felt. They were interested only in my physical presence. Acceptance without undue criticism would prove to be the bedrock of a lifelong friendship, a reality I would find equally true with people.

A month into the job, a new stallion was brought onto the farm to be trained for the show ring. He was a fancy, expensive, and beautiful horse, and he was full of himself, as stallions often are. Entering his stall to clean his sawdust bedding soon after his arrival and aware of any stud's volatility, I took a lead line and tied his head to the iron ring hanging on a side wall of his stall before beginning. As I worked, I gradually became aware that he was studying me in a way no horse or human ever had. He pulled against the rope in order to turn his head toward me and rolled his eyes to follow my motions, the whites showing around his dark pupils. I was reminded of the way a lifeguard might lower his head and peer over the top of his sunglasses to get a better look at girls in tiny beachwear. If he'd been one of those boys at school, I would have known he was flirting with me.

Perhaps in part because the boys at school rarely singled me out for attention, I was flattered by his interest. Continuing my routines, I stole repeated glances to see if my admirer was still eyeing me. It was quite a surprise when one of my peeks discovered his interest had taken the form of an erection. My first instinct was to look around to see if anyone else had noticed. Reassured that the horse and I were alone, I continued working and watching. I was surprised to find that the harder I worked and the more I sweated, the more excited the horse became. Finally he began flinging his penis against his stomach, a form of masturbation common among stallions. I blushed and pretended not to notice but I was fascinated enough to take my time with the stall before finally untying the stud and slipping from his stall.

> *Just to the rear of the barn—there he was, the black stallion. He was huge, a behemoth. A stable hand named Clint held him close to the halter by a lead line. The stallion shifted his weight and tried to crane his neck, and his hide rippled in the sunlight. Clint's dark face was already glistening with sweat from the exertion of leading him from the stable to this point. Now the stallion began to snort and jerk his head about. Clint, who was a big man and at least twenty-five years younger than Charlie, had his hands full. The mighty First Draw had made his trip to the breeding barn many times and knew exactly what was coming.*
>
> Tom Wolfe, *A Man in Full*

THE STALLION WAS my responsibility for about half a year. During that time, my periods began. Every time I cycled, the stallion announced my hormonal state to the world by his agitated reaction to my presence. Eventually others noticed the horse's flirtation. The farm master told me to smack the stud and give him a firm "No!" when he began showing his admiration, but I rarely did. The presence and effect of pheromones was something they hadn't taught in health class at school; the horse's uninhibited response gave me an insight into what was going on inside those boys I watched from a curious distance within my own herd.

My barn admirer always remained under control and I never felt threatened or endangered by him. Over time I began to see some humor in the situation. When I groomed him, he would nicker softly, telling me how much he enjoyed my touch. I found myself giggling over my brushes and wondering whether I would ever evoke the same undisguised pleasure in a boy-stallion of my own kind or whether I would experience it myself. In the presence of the randy horse, it became possible to imagine both possibilities. Horses had piqued my senses from earliest childhood; now, on the brink of womanhood, this one was indicating the road where the merely sensory evolved into something new and far more powerful.

At eighteen, I began working the Keeneland and Fasig-Tipton yearling sales, where some of the best and most promising Thoroughbreds are auctioned every season to buyers who gathered from all over the world. My job was to prepare and show yearlings in order to garner the best price in the sales ring. I normally met the youngsters a few months prior to the sales, when I began conditioning them as athletes through lengthy walks on a long lead line and teaching them manners in the barn and in the open. My first task was to gain their trust and train them to work with me as a partner when they were taken away from their pals— a bond that would keep them focused in the presence of thousands of noisy people. If I performed my job well, the yearling finding himself in this stressful situation would look to me as his alpha mare for security and direction. He would do his best to stand quietly and calmly at my request and to present himself as a well-mannered, good-looking prospect worthy of much more attention than his cohorts who showed up disheveled and unruly.

For weeks before the sale, I rubbed the horses' coats to a smooth, slick finish, pulled their manes to a perfect length that accentuated their long neck muscles, moisturized each

strand of their tails to hang down evenly and move grace-
fully with their walk. I trimmed ears, muzzle, and fetlocks;
oiled hooves to the high gleam of a pair of new spats. Every
preparation was both a means and an end: a means to fetch-
ing top dollar but also a satisfying indulgence in sensory
pleasure for both me and the young animals.

July evenings in Kentucky are notoriously hot and
sticky. The auction pavilion steams with perspiration and
cigar smoke intermingled with the fragrance of hot roast
beef and hops. When manure from a nervous young horse
hits the ground, a valet in an immaculate white coat with a
broom and a waste tin materializes to whisk it away, though
often not before its scent adds its weight to the already
heavy air. At the crowded bars, horse people keep the bar-
tenders busy splashing relief from the heat and tension
over fast-melting squares of ice. The cadence of accents
from the Middle East, Asia, England, Ireland, France, and
other distant lands mixes with the hiss of whispers into an
alluring, foreign melody. The whole place reeks of the
money and raw power crammed between its walls.

When I was working the sales, there were only a few female horse handlers, and we were appraised with the same
calculated lust directed at the fillies and colts. The attention swept me back into my first paying job as I felt those
large stallion eyes on me once more. One by one the handlers walked their yearlings up and back the bluestone
path, then stood their animals square while buyers exam-
ined them from all sides and ran a hand up a leg or two to
check the auction lot's soundness for racing. Sharing the
spotlight amid the smells and sounds and sensations gave
rise to my own animal instincts. No longer did I giggle as I
had in the stallion's stall over the sensuous pleasures that

others took and that I was beginning to desire for myself. How could I? I loved horses. From my earliest days in the barn at Hartland, they had brought my senses to life.

I have wondered sometimes if it is the beauty of a running horse that brings so many people of so many kinds to such a makeshift amphitheatre as this is, or if it is the magnetism of a crowd, or if it is only the banal hope of making an easy shilling? Perhaps it is none of these. Perhaps it is the unrecognized expectation of holding for an instant what primordial sensations can be born again in the free strength of flashing flanks and driving hooves beating a challenge against the ground.

Beryl Markham, *West With the Night*

OBSESSED AS POPULAR culture is with sex, it's easy to get the idea that *sensuality* primarily means *sexuality*. Horses know better, and, if we let them, they're happy to teach us new and varied pleasures to be taken from our senses. Horses are natively sensual beings. They don't think about how to be sexy or how to feel good about themselves physically: they don't depend on perfume and diamonds to be magnetic. They simply live fully in their bodies and their surroundings.

A horse is aware of its body at the most detailed level. He stands with his rump to the fierce wind, his tail tucked between his legs to channel the chill around and away from his body. He lowers his head. In extremes of temperature, he preserves his energy by standing still, preferably huddled within a group, and avoiding unnecessary movement. He works out instinctively. A horse doesn't require a gym to be strong or a whirlpool to relax. He takes care of his body by running in the pasture, rearing to box with another playful soul, rolling in the dirt, and standing and shaking the dust off from head to tail in a way that releases any tension or knots in his muscles.

Sitting bareback astride a horse, touching his warm sides along the full length of our legs, feeling movements up the length of our backs and into our heads, sensing in our hands as we hold the reins, we tap into the physical nature of the horse and become aware of our bodies the way a horse is. Increasing our body awareness increases our ability to experience the world sensually.

We can begin with the breathing. When we pause to draw air deeply into the lungs, we lift the diaphragm, open the ribs, and rush oxygen to the spine, into the back of the neck, and along all the extremities. Relaxed, deep breathing is an instant pick-me-up for all our senses because it replenishes every cell. We don't have to flare our nostrils the way horses do, but we can follow their example of breathing deeply enough to fuel every muscle for movement.

We can improve our posture. Any of us who suffered through posture class as adolescents (whoever could forget the book-on-the-head routine?) may have lumped the concept together with girdles and corsets as someone else's bad idea of how we ought to look. In reality, posture is simply a description of how we align the spine. Proper spinal alignment is desirable and healthful. It allows us to use all the limbs and parts that connect with the spine in a fluid and easy manner. Riding instructors are legendary for hammering their students to sit up and sit straight, producing a mannequinlike posture and a horse who feels tension and resistance to his every move. The whole picture is forced and fraught with the potential for accident, in or out of the saddle. It's not easy to enjoy our physical lives if we have pain, as often happens when we don't manage ourselves so that our spines line up in a natural way, curving and straightening where they should.

Because my Theo is aging, she is at risk to develop the sagging back that signals disuse and poor spinal alignment in a horse. I take her through regular stretching exercises as one precaution to avoid this development. I take myself through them, too. Stretching improves my general fitness and gives me the muscle tone I need to maintain my spine in a healthy manner. Every aspect of body awareness feeds my sensual life.

There was a rhythm to the canter. Up, forward, down; up, forward, down. It soon became pleasant. The broad warm rump felt good beneath her. The pounding was diminished, cushioned by the horse's muscles and the springiness of his hindquarter joints . . . The ridden horse was a marvel, diminishing space.

Morgan Llewelyn, *The Horse Goddess*

DANCING IS HOW I ride without a horse.

During the awkward early teen years, dance was only one more source of discomfort. One parent or another carpooled me and my girlfriends to a dreary church reception hall where we joined other nervous adolescents in regulation coats and ties, white gloves and patent-leather shoes. The classes reminded me of my first riding lessons, where we walked and circled and learned how to stop and go. They might have been necessary steps to skill but they offered nothing that inspired my awakening senses.

In time, the classes ended and I moved on to the less-structured dance of sock hops and school formals. Under revolving lights that splashed color on the walls of school gyms and cafeterias, I found a joy in moving on the dance floor that compared only to the liquid motion of riding. By my junior year of high school, I finally began to catch up physically and socially with the other girls. I had a boyfriend who was a smooth and sensuous dancer, a show-horse kind of guy who moved with the certainty that eyes followed him. Entering a makeshift ballroom for a special dance at his side gave me the same charge as sliding a freshly polished boot into the stirrup before a big competition. I could smell the sweat and feel the rising warmth as I moved with my stallion partner into the swaying crowd. I was reminded of Kentucky breeding barns, where the tang of freshly shaken straw and horse sweat lingered in the air and where suggestive whinnies and guttural sounds made a music all their own. In a fitted turquoise sheath, high heels, and sparkling crystal earrings, I was a horse again and ready to perform an extended trot across the diagonal. I didn't have to think about where to step or how to move any more than I had to think about how to make a horse stop or go. Together, my stallion and I rode the waves of music far into the night.

Dancing and riding remain connected today. On the occasions when I have the opportunity to dance the night away, I feel the same vitality within my body as when I compete on a cross-country course with Theo. In the intense physical exertion of the dance, I release any mixed feelings rumbling inside of me. I become clear and focused on the insatiable energy the ancients called *mare-fire*. The music moves me and I experience the same anticipation that approaching the starting box on my horse gives me. I am ready to rock and roll.

To horse people, riding and dancing are variations on the same theme. Both originate in the kinetic energy that stimulates the senses more than the mind. Whether riding or dancing, we feel and sense rather than analyze and rationalize. Dance even figures into our equine vocabulary. A number of riding exhibitions worldwide are termed "dancing with horses." Dressage is often referred to as "ballet with a horse." When a rider and horse are working together, they might be described as a "Ginger Rogers and Fred Astaire." Newcomers to riding do well to think in the imagery of music and dance as they learn. I love dancing with other horse people because it's as if we are out on a high-spirited ride together on the downs of Aintree. Dancing a hot salsa, I imagine this is how it would feel to ride in England's Grand National Steeplechase with dozens of horses running and jumping their hearts out. Slow-dancing in the arms of a partner, I am on a horse easing into a soft and smooth canter.

He [the white horse] moved like a dancer, which is not surprising: a horse is a beautiful animal, but it is perhaps most remarkable because it moves as if it always hears music.

Mark Helprin, *A Winter's Tale*

ALTHOUGH I DISCOVERED the link between sensory awareness and riding in my mid-twenties, I learned the full implications of body awareness for my sensual life only after I ignored the warning signs too long.

Several years after my first discoveries, chronic horse-lessness drove me to seek new ways to experience my power as an athlete and a woman. I was working full time every day and dancing every night, but my body and senses craved another physical outlet. I'd been a good runner in high school track. Now I began to run in the amateur races staged by charities and running clubs in towns everywhere. I was a sprinter at heart. I thought of myself as a horse who was made for a five-furlong race. Because there were no five-eighths-of-a-mile races in competition, my coach told me, "Let's just think of a long race as a series of short races all strung together." This is how my training for road running began.

For almost two years, I ran races monthly over the winding two-lane roads of the Delaware countryside and the streets of mid-Atlantic beach towns. I always ran an extremely fast first mile, then maintained a steady speed for the rest of the race. As with riding and dancing, I ran to feed my senses. I savored the sensation of fitness and power racing gave me. The salt of my own sweat seasoned my tongue and the chills that racked me after a race or hard training run confirmed that I'd pushed my limits.

By the time I turned thirty, I was living in New Jersey, where I administered a race and breeding horse partnership, trained six horses on the side, ran road races on a regular basis, and rode without horses at dance clubs all night. To top off the demands I was placing upon myself, I took twice-weekly dressage lessons in preparation for the day when I hoped to own a horse of my own. What I was not doing was being aware of my body and preparing it for all of this work. At my desk one morning, I felt unfamiliar spasms in my upper back. When I tried to stretch them away, my muscles clenched and wouldn't release. At first I was able to manage a grim laugh of denial, but, as the pain spread, I became incapable of all movement and the laughter was gone.

I was diagnosed with a compression fracture of the spine and spent the next three weeks virtually immobilized. It was torture to move and torture not to move, but the episode took me to a higher level of sensory awareness. I had taught myself to hear the messages my body gave to horses, but I was deaf to the messages my body addressed to itself. Now what I heard was that my body needed more and better attention if I wanted to enjoy my senses to the fullest. The time had come to start listening.

It is funny how long it sometimes takes to recognize something that's right under our nose. I had been training horses for years by this time. I knew that horses rarely push themselves to the point of injury. Sure, they have accidents, and some of them have conformation flaws that give them pain. But because horses live fully within their bodies and senses, they know just how much stress their bones and muscles can take and they abide healthily within those limits. Left to their own good devices and sound internal systems, horses live contentedly; only when an aggressive race jockey or an overzealous show rider is added to the equation is a horse prone to override its innate sense of self-preservation to the point of severe injury.

I knew I could simply rest up until my back relaxed and then pick up the old pace, at least until the next injury, but I finally had grasped the wisdom of the horse's respect for a body's limits. I began to understand the need to live my life consciously. I delved into the holistic relationship between diet and performance and treating my muscles to daily stretching and toning. I strove to maintain a level of physical activity that was in sync with the level of my fitness. I took the body awareness I was developing in riding and tried to apply it across the full range of my life. These measures moved me to a new level of sensuality, closer to the one a horse lives with every breath it takes.

Although my relationship with horses has changed over the years, my sensory connection with them is a constant that links every horse, every ride, and every event of today to the ones that came before it and the ones that are still to come. Horses reward every sense, even taste. A cool drink of water never tastes better than after a hard ride, but, for me, no sense awakens my memories of horses more than the sense of smell. With a whiff of liniment, I revisit the showgrounds of the Lexington Junior League Horse Show and meet a spectacular equine star. A sweat-soaked saddle pad takes me on forgotten trail rides to amazing views. Fragrant roses and mint sprigs never fail to bring back a Kentucky Derby Day.

The barn where I board my Theo does not smell like the barns of Kentucky, where the tang of burley tobacco that hung inside them before they were turned over to horses still lingers. Theo's barn is a newer environment. No breeding or foaling takes place there, and the scents are the fresh ones of horses who have just worked or been washed. All the same, my senses come alive when I step through its door. The crimping in the mare's oats releases a perfume of open fields and brisk breezes; the cedar and pine in her bedding bring the forest into a barren lot. She tears stalks of clover and long grass clippings from the packed flakes of hay; the crunch of her effort opens holes in the barn's silence.

The blankets that keep Theo warm during the winter night are hung every morning on a hook outside her stall, allowing the moisture that collects during her sleeping hours to evaporate. I see the nightwear as I approach her door and notice the soft underdown of her coat that has collected on the rough wool. I know she is well, and so am I.

COMMITMENT

Through the hayfields, over the soft mountain paths, along the muddy or stony narrow road, in the winter through deep snow, over half-frozen clods as sticky as rubber, over ice or through melting snow, treading cautiously, setting down each hoof as if the spot were previously calculated, briskly and merrily the horse moves off from the lonely cottage, down the precipitous slopes. A mobile cradle, it carries a little child to the distant church, to the christening. And it serves the Hucul all his life, from the cradle onward; until, at last, a priest rides on an exhausted and weary horse with drooping head, across the mountains to a cottage high up in the upland, to render the last service to a soul about to depart.

Stanislaw Vincenz, On the High Uplands: Sagas, Songs, Tales and Legends of the Carpathians

*N*ikoli's First is a Kentucky-bred Thoroughbred mare: bay, 16.2 hands, 1,200 pounds. She was born
January 11, 1982, a daughter of the sire Nikoli and the dam
Destiny's Reward, who owed half her genes to the good
racehorse Executioner. She made sixteen starts as a three-
and four-year-old, including one win and two second-
place finishes. It's been years since the mare has been
called anything but Theodora—Theo for short.

I met Theo when she was fourteen and I was forty. She
had been turned out to pasture after a two-year effort to
breed her had proven unsuccessful. Her mane was long and
shaggy, her tail brittle and broken, her belly round, and her
back showed incipient sag. Even so, blood tells. She was a
beautiful horse with a reserve of energy. I didn't own a horse
at the time but I exercised a number of them for other people. I never thought much about the fading mare during my
visits to the farm where she lived, other than to note she was
a particularly high-strung Thoroughbred with a neurotic

streak. I caught the gossip around the barn that she was difficult to deal with and disliked men.

I had been riding an old Appaloosa named Apples for a few months when he went lame and needed a break in our training routine. Helen Junkin, the woman who owned both the farm and Theo, asked what I was going to ride while the gelding was laid up. I told her I didn't know, that I thought I might start looking for a horse to buy. With my growing network of connections, I assumed I could find a nice one for little money.

Helen offered to help me find a horse of my own and puzzled aloud over her own particular quandary: what to do with Theo. The lovely Thoroughbred was past her athletic prime but repeated efforts to breed her had failed. Helen was unwilling to invest more time and effort into vain hope, and the horsewoman had a new horse she was working with actively. All the same, Theo had once been the star of the farm, and Helen still loved the mare; she simply lacked the desire and energy needed to put the horse back into regular work.

It took a while for Helen and me to figure out we each held the missing piece to the other's puzzle. In the meantime, I actively searched for a horse of my own. At one point, I was so close to a purchase that a check was tucked in my back pocket. Then I learned the gelding I had chosen had failed the prepurchase veterinary exam. I was forced to begin all over again.

On one of my visits to Helen's farm, I was recounting my horse-shopping frustrations to the horsewoman when she suddenly asked, "Would you like to ride Theo while you're looking around?"

I was shocked, hesitant, and excited. Helen had bought

Theo off the racetrack and became only her second owner, a bit of a rarity. Racehorses can go through several owners during and after their racing careers, which often deprives them of consistent care and management. Her five years with her first owner gave her a good foundation for a healthy life. Although she'd already raced for two years, Theo was exceptionally sound in her limbs and balanced in her body, and Helen had retrained her as a show horse. The two had teamed up in many horse trials and dressage competitions, once bringing home the bronze medal in third-level dressage from the United States Dressage Federation—an impressive accomplishment. Theo and Helen had been together since the mare was a five-year-old. These two ladies knew each other intimately. Helen's attentions might have shifted to her new horse but Theo still owned her heart. I was deeply touched.

Helen spent three days preparing Theo for our formal introduction—cleaning her up, pulling her mane, combing out her tail, and riding her for the first time in three years. As I sat on one of the railroad ties that bordered the sand arena on the first day I rode the mare, I watched Helen school the horse for a few minutes and couldn't help admiring the way Theo moved. She might have been a little rough around the edges, but she was still a big, gorgeous Thoroughbred who had done many things in her life. The trouble was that the sourness in her disposition was profound. There was an unmistakable anger about her. She was fussy about the saddle position, fussy about moving forward, cranky about life.

Helen stayed with me as I mounted the mare and began walking. The horse remained nervous, but I felt important high up on the beautiful creature. She had been out of work for three years yet her canter was comfortable, rhythmic, and sure. A tug-of-war started up in my heart between the allure of the mare's athleticism and the perversity of her temperament. The only thing I knew for sure was that I wanted to ride her again.

Commitment, like loyalty, is no longer as prized as it once was. A reader doesn't have to turn more than a couple pages of any daily newspaper before coming across some factoid about a company downsizing and forcing workers out, divorced fathers failing to pay child support, drug mothers abandoning their babies, or some other symptom that the threads of our loyalty aren't as tightly woven as they used to be. Yet commitment remains as vital to relationships as it ever was. It's a bit like gravity: an invisible force that prevents us from floating apart in the open spaces of our lives.

When I agreed to ride Theo—when any of us chooses to take a horse of our own—a commitment of great magnitude was made. Horses drain our time and our wallets. They make calls on us that must be met even when equally pressing calls are coming from elsewhere. They possess temperaments that require nurturing as urgently as their bodies require sustenance. In domesticating the horse, we have made it dependent on us and fragile in its dependency. A woman who wants to explore the territory of commitment and claim it for her own may find no better instructor than a horse.

If Theo had been human, I imagine she would have been a retired ballet dancer who had enjoyed a respectable career but that for reasons she wouldn't go into ended too soon. Taking me a little into her confidence, she might have confessed that she disliked her sedate new life and longed to be active again. It would have been impossible not to notice the beauty of her face and form, but I would also have detected pain and flashes of anger. Perhaps she would have hunched over her porcelain teacup, her body tight and twisted in a way I would never have expected from an artist and athlete. Her hair and clothes would have been a little awry, an eccentricity that would have surprised me because her professional life had been one of physical perfection. I would have found her intelligent and sensitive but oddly inhibited—a woman who spoke her mind with hesitation, as if she were afraid of being herself or making mistakes, except at unpredictable moments when torrents of venom escaped. I would have viewed her as something of a lost soul.

Why is Parsifal such a challenge? He is a heavyweight boxer that I try to turn into a ballet dancer. His father, Pastor, was not a lightweight Luso, rather a strongly built stallion for his type. His mother was an Irish middleweight hunter, a bay by name Electra. They produced Parsifal, and to prove it can be done with any horse if you know how, I try to prove my point with Parsifal. To round the spine and lighten the forehand to get ballet from my boy is already a task that boggles the mind, to say nothing of the horse of work that must be put in from the start. Start I have, and will continue for as long as I can.

Patricia Findlay, *Parsifal Perhaps: A Classical Courtship*

FROM THE FIRST day I rode her, I worked exclusively with Theo. I sensed that the only way I would gain her trust and build a relationship for the two of us together was by easing her physical pain and helping her soul find a comforting, accepted place in the world.

Helen would sit on the deck of her farmhouse on the hill, watching us work and experiment together. I developed a routine meant to relax and reassure the mare and to retrain her body to become aware of its movement. The routine began with grooming and massage in the barn and the field, followed by stretching exercises when I encouraged her to reach out and around to get a carrot or an apple treat in a way that lengthened her tight muscles. Then we moved on to ground work in the sand arena and, finally, to low-stress riding. With every step I talked to her, telling her what a good girl she was and how happy she made me. In retrospect, those first engagements of ours weren't so different from the beginning of a relationship with any new friend. There was no need to rush. I didn't expect to win the mare's affection overnight. I worked at maintaining a level head in the face of her aloofness, and I certainly never resorted to harsh words or actions. I simply committed myself to giving the relationship all the time it needed to assume its fullest potential.

We seemed to be making progress until one afternoon, about two weeks into our association. I was brushing her girth area when, without warning or provocation, she lashed out and kicked me. The blow just grazed my thigh but it was still hard enough to sting and bruise. What's more, it had been aimed and fired with precision. The horse clearly was directing her anger specifically at me. Even though I was the one person who was trying to help her, she wanted to hurt me.

For an instant, I wanted to strike back. Instead, I stepped away, took a deep breath, and looked into her eyes. Horses and humans are alike in developing defenses that give them a sense of safety when the world feels inhospitable. Those who love these unfortunates unconditionally endure the most abuse because they are the ones willing to reach out and touch what hurts. Theo was behaving as many damaged people do when she lashed out: She was testing my commitment. Fortunately, I knew from experience that the reward for putting up with the stings and the bruises is the joy of seeing a buried soul emerge.

I shifted to a stern voice and said, "Theo, please, do not do that again." Many horses hold tension in their jaw and mouth, and I had been taught a technique to help release that stress. I tried it then, massaging her mouth with my hand as if I were rolling and softening an orange before peeling it. A hand in an angry horse's mouth may seem dangerous, but it brings the animal a pleasure and comfort that signals the handler is capable of taking away her pain and replacing it with relief. After a few moments, I resumed grooming as if nothing had happened. Theo didn't object further and we went on to enjoy a good workout.

In this manner, gingerly and one layer at a time, I lifted the mare's defenses. To our routines, I gradually added small acts of kindness to show I understood her. Helen told me the horse was a mud maven and loved to roll in puddles. I started dipping her bit into her water bucket before putting it in her mouth. She seemed to welcome this thoughtfulness by opening her mouth gently and chewing the bit as I inserted it, an improvement over her previous tight-lipped attitude.

There were many times in the beginning when Theo stopped abruptly, pinned her ears, and kicked out or bucked. I did not punish her. Instead, I stroked her neck and talked to her, asking her to keep moving by alternating my legs against her sides and releasing my lower back. The feeling I tried to convey to her was one of freedom in her movement and throughout her body. I used no restraint or pressure to direct her, only encouragement. In the canter, I stood in the stirrups, lifting my seat out of the saddle to make my body as weightless as possible on her back and to encourage her to feel the glorious freedom of moving forward. This was a horse born to move, yet she was stuck in her body and often stopped and complained by kicking out or refusing to go forward. During these "stuck moments" I stroked her neck and talked to her, gently asking her to walk forward. Then we walked until we found her sense of calm again.

When the girl came as she always did and kneaded
the new dead hairs from his bright coat with supple fingers and ran the soft body-brush over him, he turned his
head and watched her, accepting the soothing stroke of
her hand, but he knew that the old anger was in him
again. It had welled up in his heart until now it burst
and made him whirl round and catch her slender back
with his teeth, biting until the brush dropped from her
hand, flinging her bodily against the far wall of the box.
She lay there huddled in the trampled bedding for a long
time, and he stood over her, trembling, not touching her
with any of his feet. He would not touch her. He would
have killed any living creature that touched her then, but
he did not know why this was so.

After a while the girl moved and then crawled out of
the box and he pawed through the bedding to the earthen
floor, tossing his head up and down, letting the anger run
out of him.

But the girl was there again, in the stable, the next
day. She cleaned it as she had cleaned it each other day
and her touch on his body was the same, except there was
a new firmness in it, and Camciscan knew, without knowing, that his strength, his anger, and his loneliness at last
were challenged. . . .

Beryl Markham, *West With the Night*

IT TOOK A long time to convince Theo that I would be there for her regardless of her tantrums. It was perhaps six months before I felt I was beginning to break through, and, even then, the changes were subtle. I remember an afternoon when we were schooling outside the farm at a nearby arena. After our workout, I needed to dismount in order to open and close a few gates on our way home. Once the gates were all closed behind us and we were out on the dirt road, Theo swung her head high in the air and pranced sideways, snorting and calling to her friends far away. I had to find a way to get back on, but she was clearly not in the mood to stand still and wait for me. Her mind was elsewhere and her body wanted to follow. There in the road, I returned to our barn and arena routines—talking, walking up and down the lane, making subtle S-shapes, reclaiming her focus. Eventually I was able to maneuver her near a fence where I could climb up and mount. We pranced with the gait of a horse heading for the racetrack all the way home. I could feel her at the edge of an explosion and an earnest impulse to get rid of me. However, just enough trust had been established in our young relationship to hold her with me. I admired her effort. She was stressed and tempted to misbehave but she was handling her tension in a new and more positive way.

This incident opened a window for me into Theo's soul. The massages and ground exercises and riding in the barn and arena were all fine, but her trust when we were alone on open roads was the most crucial element if we were to enjoy life to its fullest as a team. This would take time, honesty, and my determination not to give up. In the meantime, I could expect her to keep testing and I would have to teach her that I could be counted on to endure.

I must not forget to thank the difficult horses, who made my life miserable, but who were better teachers than the well-behaved school horses who raised no problems.
Alois Podhajsky, Director of the Spanish Riding School, 1939

LATER IN OUR first year together, Theo and I began to compete; at those shows, she demonstrated how far she'd come. We trailered to the first show with Apples, her long-time buddy. As long as the Appaloosa remained nearby, Theo was quiet and well behaved. However, when I shifted her to the warm-up arena, she became concerned and distracted, and when Apples's owner took him out of sight altogether, the mare completely lost control. She reared straight up in the air, taking me by surprise and alarming many onlookers. Perhaps she was just standing up in an effort to spot her buddy; I couldn't know. I took a deep breath, focused on calming my adrenal rush, and asked her to move forward. She listened and progressed through our warm-up. We won our class but, for me, the biggest victory was Theo overcoming her anxieties and performing despite the stress of the gelding's disappearance.

At the farm, Theo and I continued our old routines, to which I now added jumping lessons. Theo had not jumped in more than eight years. A natural athlete, she took to the challenge with ease even though she was still wrestling with issues I couldn't diagnose. On the days when she couldn't even make turns without stopping in pain, we settled for a long walk. At the same time, I took her on trails farther and farther from home, extending our boundaries. She loved these outings. No longer did she perform her nervous, silly jigs. Into the woods, over streams and bridges and small jumps, through wide-open meadows and down long shaded lanes we went—walking, trotting, and galloping together in our growing mutual confidence.

As Theo's spirit flourished in the warmth of my commitment and her own hard work, I found in her a sister. It wasn't just that I understood her; I felt she understood me. When our eyes met, I felt a start of recognition. We were getting to know each other deep below the surfaces. I could see myself in her. I'm impatient; so is she. If I was busy talking to someone, she would take a canvas blanket off its hook on the wall of her stall and throw it on the floor. If I turned to find out what was happening, she gave me a look as if to say *ex-CUUUSE me*. She was like the special friend whose moodiness is tolerable when nobody else's would be, just because there was something special about her. When she gave me a horse hug for the first time, it was an unforgettable embrace. Standing by my side, she brought her head around me, like a mare cuddling her foal, gently pulling my weight into the deepest curve of her neck. It was a rush of loving acceptance.

My reward for committing myself to the difficult mare outstripped anything I imagined in those early days together. As Helen observed my patience and compassion no matter what Theo threw at me, she began to consider letting the horse go for good.

Not long after my second competition with Theo, my husband and I made the decision to move to Colorado. Tom had received a tantalizing job offer, and I was ready to leave the East Coast for an entirely new adventure in the Rocky Mountains. I told Helen we would be moving in a couple of months and said no more.

One afternoon she came down to the barn while I was

grooming Theo. Settling onto the top step of the barn's doorway, she watched in silence for a few minutes. I knew something was on her mind and continued brushing as I waited for it to come out. Finally she spoke.

"How would you like to take Theo with you?" she asked simply.

I was forty-one years old. I had been a horse nearly from birth but had never owned a horse as accomplished as Theo or one who had touched me so deeply. Helen's attachment to the mare ran so profound that she had commissioned an immense oil portrait of the horse. Theo was a gift I would never be able to repay. Helen attached no strings to her offer; yet, in accepting it, I would be making an enormous commitment. Not only were there financial and time considerations, but I would be assuming an obligation to accept Theo as she was—which was far from perfect—and to give her the best quality of life possible despite those imperfections. Helen and I both thought her offer over for many weeks. In the end, I accepted. Theo's Jockey Club registration papers and all the files that documented the mare's ownership would travel west with the horse.

Tom and I moved to Colorado in September, but Theo didn't leave Virginia until late October. I had thought October would be a good time to ship her—before Colorado's snow season set in—but I was still a beginner in the Rocky Mountain weather department. The first snow of a thirty-inch storm began falling on Denver and the plains the day my mare left Virginia; by the time she reached Kansas, it still blocked the interstate highways. The horse spent nearly two and a half days standing in an eighteen-wheeler. The trailer drivers called to say they were offering the horses water and feed every few hours, but I had no way of knowing how the ordeal was trying her high-strung soul. All I could do was wait.

Theo arrived in Boulder four days after she left Virginia. She was generally healthy but the trip had taken its toll. She had lost a tremendous amount of weight and her head hung low. The drivers told me she'd taken no water during the entire hold-up in Kansas. Theo had retreated behind her defenses again.

Inside her new spacious stall, I tucked her in with loads of hay, fresh water, and some grain. She had a snotty nose, which was not surprising given the enclosed, tight conditions she had been in with other horses. The veterinarian met me at the barn first thing the next morning for a thorough examination. The vet prescribed vitamins, administered antibiotic shots, and dressed a wound Theo had rubbed above her tail, probably from leaning up against the wall of the trailer most of the trip.

Over the next three weeks, we began again. I walked the horse in hand, massaged and medicated her, and slowly returned to our routines. She recovered and soon showed signs of enjoying her new life in Colorado. In the large pasture, breathing the dry, fresh air and cantering under the wide-open blue sky, she regained her weight and her spirits and our partnership revived.

Normally I ride Theo during the day, but I've gone through spells when the rest of life pushed my riding time into the darkening hours of the evening. One night not long ago, Theo and I were the only ones at the stable. I turned the lights on in the indoor arena and we found ourselves together and alone in a large open space. After our warm-up lunging (exercising a horse on a long line in a circle around you) session, I released her to roam around the arena while I put away her lunge line and prepared to ride. Curious to see how my mare would handle the arena's big emptiness, I wandered to its far end, leaving her to choose my company or her own. She was preoccupied with her reflection in a mirror on the wall and didn't notice my departure.

Just as I reached the distant end, Theo turned and called to me with a nicker, then broke into a gallop across the sand until she came to a dead stop in front of me. As I laid a hand on her shoulder, the mare let out a big breath of relief. She had felt a moment of loneliness and insecurity and had run to me for reassurance. She might not know the word "commitment," but she knew the sensation of it. As I mounted her, she dropped her head and stretched her back as if to say *Thanks for being there for me, Mary. I feel much better now.*

These were some of Christine's happiest moments with her horse, and Jet seemed to enjoy them too. For the day's work was done, and in the peace of the evening there seemed to be a quiet understanding between the girl and her horse, who watched her with a dreamy and trustful gaze. Sometimes, tired though she was, Christine could hardly bear to leave Jet. She would stand gazing at him with pride and love, delighting in the slope of his shoulder beneath the tattered old rug, the Arab quality of his small head, the carriage of his fine silken tail, and the perfect conformation of quarters and hocks and "tea-cup" feet.

Marjorie Stace, "Racing Rivals"
from *Horse and Pony Stories for Girls*

CREATIVITY

And if a man should see
The horse's magical face,
He would tear out his own impotent tongue
And give it to the horse. For
This magical creature is surely worthy of it.
Then we should hear words.
Words large as apples. Thick
As honey or buttermilk.
Words which penetrate like flame
And, once within the soul, like fire in some hut,
Illuminate its wretched trappings.
Words which do not die
And which we celebrate in song.

Nikolai Alekseevich Zabolotsky,
"The Face of the Horse"
from The Poetry of Horses

*I*n my early twenties, Maggie appeared on my horizon.

She was a college classmate who materialized like a rogue horse on a mountaintop and came down to call me away from my herd. As a curious young mare, I followed her into unfamiliar canyons and forests to see what lay beyond my own territory. She showed me how to select leaves and buds with the best taste and texture, how to ring my tail and shake my mane in the cool breezes, how to prance and snort. But when I asked her to come and graze and lie in the sun with my herd, she shook her head with boredom and nudged me to trot away with her instead.

Maggie was from Las Vegas and unlike anyone I had ever known. She was tall and slender, and her dress and manner were dramatic. She was chic by my country-girl standards: She smoked extra-long cigarettes that she held as if they were priceless slivers of fine crystal and she disdained the blue jeans most of us wore. She applied her dark red lipstick heavy and wet and painted her long fingernails—even her toenails—to match. She was seventeen hands tall barefoot, but she still wore stilettos whenever she went out, a sleek greyhound at her side.

No doubt about it: Maggie was not a typical University of Kentucky student. She was an alpha mare living in the wild. When she took shelter, it was in a cave of fancifulness beyond the imagination of a tame young horse like myself. Sheer floral fabrics billowed at her windows instead of the typical student decor of sagging venetian blinds or a faded old bed sheet. Scarves she had tossed into the air draped over chairs and sofas in a random design. Rugs in a multitude of textures and colors checkered the floor and big tasseled pillows leaned against furniture. Vines dripped from every corner, and old gilt-framed wall mirrors bounced reflections across the two small rooms of her cave. Maggie didn't own a television; her electronic amusement came from a large stereo and speakers that always held a mess of ashtrays brimming with spent incense sticks and lipstick-stained cigarette butts. The scent of old incense lingered and mingled with her perfume, much the way whiskey and cigar smoke and leather had mingled in my grandfather's car.

When I visited Maggie in her apartment, I always felt I was in a movie, a wide-eyed Bambi checking out the ice for the first time. In the untamed mare's presence, my mind raced with ideas and possibilities that never seemed to find me anywhere else. Her environment provoked and inspired me in ways I had never before experienced. It was no wonder I thought of her as a horse. Horses had always been my Muses; Maggie was the first human to sing to me as horses did, but, as a human, she could lead me down paths they didn't know.

Maggie often took me shopping and showed me how

she carefully selected special cards, books, and gifts for certain people in her life. I had never seen anyone so sensitive to the exact occasion of the gift and so adroit at putting together such a personal package. Her gifts to me were always meaningful—full of love and care. When she wrote me a note, she took the extra step of including a pressed flower or a drop of incense oil.

On our walks in the old downtown parks of Lexington, Maggie drew my attention to scents and sounds I had never noticed. She would spot a rabbit nibbling in a flower bed and make up a story about it and its life with its rabbit family. Sometimes we spent an entire day and night in her tiny cave just talking, eating, drinking, and listening to music, leaving only to go for long strolls. I was sure Maggie was one of the goddess Danu's Tuatha de Danann tribe of faeries who rode pure white horses of magnificent stature, their manes and tails plaited with bells, jewels, and flowers. She opened my eyes to a world of imaginative wonder and possibility beyond the obvious.

They had wonderful fun together when they were out, Christine pretending they were all sorts of different people. Sometimes, Jet would be a ranch horse and Christine a cowpuncher riding slack and long-legged in the saddle. And once she'd been a highwayman and Jet a mettlesome, high-spirited creature flying at full gallop across the broad heath, under the light of the moon.

The lovely thing about Jet was the way he always seemed to enter into the spirit of these games.

But there were so many other things about Jet: his turn of speed, his courage, his love of hunting; the way he drowsed on a summer afternoon and dipped his head and

blew against your hair. To Christine he was a picture-
book horse, and often, in her mind's eye, she clothed him
in crimson and gold trappings and rode him out across
the open heath, pretending he was a charger and she a
Knight in search of the Holy Grail.

Marjorie Stace, "Racing Rivals" from
Horse and Pony Stories for Girls

MAGGIE WAS THE first mare of my own kind who led me
into the landscape of imagination. Long after I'd passed
into lands far beyond her cave, I was still reimagining the
world in ways she taught me. When I returned later to places
we'd gone together, I remembered her not so much as a
woman I'd known but as a strange and magical mare, rather
like the magic horse of *1001 Arabian Nights* who would carry its
rider anywhere if only a pin in its ear was turned. Horses
bring magic into women's lives because they give our imaginations free rein. As a young girl riding a broomstick
pony, my imagination carried me into the skies even when
my broomstick Wendy Wonderful didn't. Now that I'm a
woman, my imagination continues to take wing when I ride.
On my Theo's back, I am Joan of Arc riding into battle and
Annie Oakley dazzling the queen of England in Buffalo
Bill's Wild West show. I am a goddess soaring to the heavens,
a pioneer woman crossing the Great Plains, a feudal lady
escaping the castle walls for an afternoon. There is no reality check (no little voice saying *Don't be silly. Joan of Arc is dead;*
you are Mary Dike Midkiff) because the moment I step into the
stirrup, I've already surrendered the rational to the imaginative. If the bumbling Don Quixote could be turned into
a gallant knight on the back of his nag Rozinante, all things
are possible for me in the saddle on my magnificent mount.

We all want everything to be wonderful. Every woman wants to sit upon a horse dressed in bells and go riding off through the boundless green and sensual forest.
Clarissa Pinkola Estés, *Women Who Run With the Wolves*

THE HORSE IS a catalyst for a woman's creativity because it carries us through the doors that stand between the familiar and the unfamiliar, limitations and freedom, and introduces us to experiences we might otherwise miss.

Artists Rosa Bonheur of the early nineteenth century ("The Horse Fair") and Lucy Kemp-Welch of the early twentieth century ("Black Beauty") found through their magnificent horse paintings and sculptures an expression of acceptance and freedom that had been unavailable to them as women and professionals. The horse brought their creative feminine energy to life and served as a symbol of their self-image—a metaphor for passion.

At some point in adulthood, most of us have worn a groove of sameness into our lives. We stop looking for new ways to do things because we have tried-and-true ways that are comfortable already. We stop trying on new ideas because we like the ideas we've already formed. We become less adventurous.

If we let them, horses can carry us out of the arena of sameness and into new worlds of possibility, in much the same way Maggie led me.

"The symbol of wide open spaces and freedom, synonymous with nature in a mechanised world, the horse arouses great passion and feeds our imaginations," offers Bertrand Leclair in *1001 Images of Horses*. And Richard Lewinsohn in *Animals, Men and Myths*, points out, "To the

Greek mind horses were more than mere earthbound animals; they belonged in an imaginary space. They drew Poseidon's car of the ocean, they lifted themselves on mighty
pinions into the air. Pegasus was one of these, sprung from
the head of Medusa. Before becoming allied with the
Muses he bore the poets up into the realms of fantasy."

Horses inspire language to match them, words that roll
off the tongue and tickle the imagination. *Mare-fire, coltpixie,
palfrey, courser, Ehwaz, rouncy,* and *cob; horsel, ambler, destrier* and
horse-loosed; dobbin and *gigster; bayard* and *skewbald; water horse, sea
horse, moon horse, wind horse, night horse,* and *wonder horse.* Without
knowing the meaning, we hear the drumbeat of horse
hooves in the words and see fantastic creatures race
through our minds.

In *Horses in Shakespeare's England,* Anthony Dent explains,
"[Horsemanship] had everything to do with display, with
'magnificence,' with what the modern show judge calls
'presence' in horse and rider. It was above all theatrical
and its presentation either to a select audience of the
Prince and his court or less frequently to the eyes of the
vulgar had so much in common with dramatic spectacle
that it is no wonder that the writers for the stage were
drawn time and again to the description of it."

It is no coincidence that the fantasy, power, and inspiration of horses surround us and speak to us every day in
parks, squares, city and government centers, entertainment venues and pedestrian malls; in television, movies,
and advertising; and in works of art, theater, and graphic
design. The awesome statues and sculptures of horses like
the proud chariot horses of Boadicea (Boudicca), a queen
and warrior of England in A.D. 61, touch me as I stare at
her horse's flashing mysterious eyes; the models of the

T'ang dynasty's powerful saddle horse which adorned royal gravesites for centuries and the early flying horse of the Han dynasty, fill me with wonder at how they dance even in stone. Emperor Marcus Aurelius's steed remains full of grandeur in Rome's central square even though it is worn with almost two thousand years of age; Revolutionary and Civil War bronzed horse heroes that grace cities throughout America stir in me mixed feelings of honor for their loyalty and grief for their exploitation.

Media and entertainment corporations (in a high-tech art form) have seized upon the provocative and allusive horse icon to move us. For example, Mobil Oil established Pegasus as their symbol, which stands tall as if to fly away, in a life-size neon sign atop their office skyscrapers; Budweiser delivers their messages with powerful, majestic Clydesdales; Busch beer features a black stallion rearing in a rocky mountain environment alluding to cold, raw strength; Ford's Mustang has the reputation of energy and passion associated with a wild horse; several perfume companies show us specters of women and their lovers and horses playing on our romantic fantasies of Sir Galahad or Lady Godiva; Tri-Star Film Productions begins all of their movies with a flying white horse serving as a vehicle to take us to the imaginary as we sit in our theater seats ready to escape real life.

The omnipresent horse imagery reminds me to get back to the barn to live those feelings through my hands and my senses, and know that I can realize the imaginary with my horse. Horses give us a magnificent canvas on which to capture unworldly beauty.

We brush and comb out their manes and tails, trim their ears and fetlocks, dress them up in active wear and sometimes in finery, parade them around others, and show off their talents as if they were artwork we had painted or sculpted. We can express ourselves in the breed we choose to ride or own or lease. An extremely artistic and passionate person might choose a fancy Baroque-type horse with a powerful arched neck, long mane, and high step like the Andalusian's. A woman of more modest composure might want an easygoing Quarter Horse—a horse she can feel comfortable and secure with, a partner of equal expression. Yet another woman might express herself through her athletic pursuits with her horse, giving no consideration to looks or breeding. Horses give us a hundred—a thousand!—new ways to express ourselves if only we will.

The mare with a flowing mane, which was never broke to any servile toil and labour, composed an eighth species of women. Those are they who have little regard for their husbands, who pass away their time in dressing, bathing, and perfuming; who throw their hair into the nicest curls, and trick it up with the fairest flowers and garlands. A woman of this species is a very pretty thing for a stranger to look upon, but very detrimental to the owner, unless it be a king or prince who takes a fancy to such a toy.

Simonides of Ceos, Greek lyric poet

THERE'S AN ADAGE in horse circles that if you've got a problem you can't work out, you "ask a wise old horseman." Like most sayings, this one springs from long experience and close observation. Wise old horsemen and horsewomen know what it is to circle a problem, chew on it for a while, and resolve it with a measure of wisdom—in my vet's words, to treat it with a tincture of time and patience. "Problem-solving is one of the best ways to become inventive," Adele von Rust McCormick and Marlena Deborah McCormick, a mother-daughter team who write about their use of horses in psychotherapy, say in their book, *Horse Sense and the Human Heart*: "Facing an immediate dilemma stretches our minds and teaches us to reach into other dimensions." This kind of resourcefulness is a form of creativity that horses constantly call from us.

If we work closely with a horse, inevitably his or her behaviors and movements will come to express our own natures and imaginations. I regard the fact that my Theo has become such a cooperative partner as a reflection of the imagination I have put to work in dealing with her problems. Horses can't help stimulating resourcefulness in us because horses don't speak our language. We like to imagine they do. We've been writing and telling stories—even making television shows—about horses that talk, for as long as we've been storytelling. But they don't talk. They signal their needs and desires with body language and changes in behavior, just as a baby or toddler does. They ask us to look to their body positions and their vital signs and to our senses, our experiences, our ancestors, and our hearts to filter through the possibilities of what they need and how we might meet that need. Like an infant, the horse suffers if we don't read the signals quickly and accurately.

Women have developed a talent for reading nonverbal cues. In most homes with a new baby, it's the father who struggles to figure out the message in a baby's wail, not the mother. It's the wife who explains her husband to his children or parents or friends, not the husband who explains the wife. Women often act as translators in human

interactions because we are innately interested in relationships, and interpreting nonverbal signals is one of the ways
we foster our connections with others. Horsewomen often
compare riding a horse to learning a foreign language, the
difference being that it is a language learned through observation and touch rather than sound and speech.

Horses have a way of polishing this instinctive knack to
a high art. The horse has simple problems that are com-
municated in complex ways because the horse can't speak.
Humans have complex problems that are capable of being
solved simply through verbal communication but often are
not because we don't always use our verbal skills to good effect. Horses compel us to develop alternative ways of reading one another and, in the process, give us an additional
language we can use effectively in the world of our human
relationships.

My husband and I have different styles in handling stress.
Occasionally he will retreat from me and disappear inside
himself to think something through. I approach the mystery
of his disappearance the same way I do with Theo's occasional remoteness. I take an inner snapshot of his life over
the previous few days and weeks and try to remember any
event or incident that might be affecting his happiness. I
mentally look at those pictures capturing the dynamics of his
environment at work, at play, and at home. I wait and watch
and occasionally ask questions that might elicit information
about the source of his distress. Usually I can isolate the
source of his pain if I take my time and allow the sore spot to
reveal itself in nonverbal ways. While I wait for the issue to
come out and get resolved, the understanding and patience
that horses have taught me gives me peace of mind. I have relied on these skills before, and they have rarely failed me.

Horses give us confidence in our resourceful natures. When women share their horse crisis stories with me, it is often with a sense of wonder and pride at what they found within themselves. A horse with colic is a dangerous situation. Death can occur with horrifying quickness if the intestine is not flushed or repaired rapidly. The horse in this danger needs a human who can conjure every imaginable strategy for getting the animal through its peril. Women discover the imaginative and creative powers within themselves when they pass through events like this.

Horses have been a source of inspiration long before this particular horsewoman set foot in a stirrup. Lamri was Muse to King Arthur, Bucephalus to Alexander the Great, Hiazum to the archangel Gabriel in the Koran. In my lifetime, I have had the privilege of meeting and touching My-My, Seattle Slew, Silver Charm, Real Quiet, Flight Time, John Henry, Secretariat, Donnerhall, Suna, Gem Twist, and Rugged Lark—all world-class earthly horses. They have all inspired me, as Maggie inspired me and as my horses Tory, Diva, Bandit, and Theo have inspired me. Every one of these equine friends taught me to stop, to settle, and to open myself to new ways of seeing and doing and living.

Beyond the barn, I enjoy decorating my house, especially by rummaging among the things I already possess and finding new and different ways to use and present them. When I do this, the process is not so different from going within myself to find new and better ways of working with Theo. When a woman spends time around a horse, she finds a flesh-and-blood Muse to sing to her soul. Mine sings not only when I'm with her but when I garden or decorate or write. The horse Muse is an equal-opportunity goddess with a voice for each one of us. I'm convinced that horses inspire us as we knit, draw, cook, paint, sing, sculpt, act, invent, or problem-solve. The mares of our physical world are sisters to the mares of our souls. When we bring them together and give them their heads, the tethers around our imaginations release and the universe is ours to roam.

I HEAR in my heart,
I hear in its ominous pulses,
All day, on the road, the hoofs of invisible horses.

Louise Imogen Guiney, from *"Wild Ride"*

JOYCE NESMITH AND PRESTO

It is a constant source of pleasure and amazement that, at a mature stage in my life, I am learning so many new things and that my teacher is a horse.

One experience stands out strongly for the way it opened my mind and captured my attention and imagination. It occurred about a year after I met Presto. I traveled to Florida during the winter circuit with some horse friends and I had the great good fortune to take a couple of riding lessons with a well-known reiner on one of his retired show horses. He put me in a round pen and had me do a few exercises. He then instructed me to trot to a particular point in the pen and to think "stop"—no aid of any kind was to be used. I was only to think "stop." Well, the horse stopped immediately when we trotted to that spot and I thought "stop." My response was— "You've signaled your horse in a way I didn't see!" So Marc told me to pick my own spot and do the same thing. We picked up a trot and I picked out a spot, and thought "stop." Sure enough, the horse stopped. It took me quite a while to figure out what happened that day and I am forever grateful to that man for the experience. It set me on a course of discovery that has provided me so much pleasure and led me to discover my passion.

Marc said two things to me that I remember well: (1) Enjoy your horse; (2) You will learn a lot about yourself in dealing with horses. Here are some examples of what I've learned.

When I first got Presto, he was what I would later call "shut down." He was described as having "concrete sides." He was unresponsive to all but the loudest of aids. On one occasion, he and I were out trail riding by ourselves on a peaceful, quiet day. I was thoroughly relaxed. I began to experiment with very soft leg pressure and was surprised to see how quickly he responded. Whispers of the rein and soft nudges immediately gave me every change of direction I asked for. That experience taught me that Presto was willing to receive and act on my requests if I asked in the right way.

What I learned from this experience was to keep an open mind; experiment; make my own judgments; and have faith in myself even if this turns out to be contrary to the opinion of "experts"—which isn't easy when you're in a new field.

Another day we were out trail riding alone. We came to a fork in the road. I looked down the right fork and Presto began to take that direction. I was only looking that way and had intended to go left, so I quickly looked to the left and Presto immediately changed his direction with no other aid or request from me other than my looking to the left. This astonished me, and taught me that he was a sensitive horse and attuned to his rider.

This moment taught me to be aware of ways that I communicate, even when I am not talking.

There is a long stretch of Hedgeland Lane that leads to Route 662 near the barn. Presto and I were recently out trail riding and we headed down that lane. Some road repair work was being done on 662 at the end of the lane with a dump truck, a tamper, and men shouting and carrying on. Presto was a little concerned about all this as we headed down the lane. He stopped. I reassured him and asked him to move forward; he did and I praised him. After a few feet he stopped again, and we repeated the process. As we moved closer to the machinery and noise, Presto became more concerned—he planted his feet firmly and when I asked him to move on he literally turned his head to look me in the face as if to say, "Are you sure *you see all that stuff going on at the end of the lane?" I talked to him some more, and he moved on. We repeated the stop, talk, head turn, and moving on twice more. Then I decided to turn around, which of course Presto was more than happy to do. What impressed me was that he clearly trusted my judgment in a situation he was not comfortable with. The other thing that I was proud of (later, when I thought about it) was that I had the good (I think) judgment to not press the situation beyond a point where I thought I would get what I asked for. There was a time when I might have pushed too far.*

I learned from this (1) that being calm and confident can help others through uncomfortable situations and (2) the importance of knowing when to stop.

Sometimes I forget to praise Presto when he does something good or that I particularly like; I just accept it as a matter of course. When I do praise him and make a fuss over something, I notice that he seems to be more willing and puts more of himself into the doing of a thing. Then I remember that everyone feels good when genuine praise is handed out—both the giver and the receiver. This reminds me to treat people the same way, and I try harder to find ways to hand out well-deserved compliments.

I admire the way horses notice details, and I try to emulate their powers of observation. I consider myself sensitive to people and the various signals they send, but any ability I have pales in comparison to what a horse notices. I've tried to become more observant of people since I began riding and to use these observations to understand their behaviors possibly prevent problems. Being around horses has made me extra-sensitive.

When I have riding lessons I concentrate and focus fully on what I am doing. Rarely do I have the luxury of concentrating so fully in other areas of my life where there are always distractions and interruptions. However, now when it is essential that I focus on something, I find it easier to ignore distractions by virtue of practicing this technique in my weekly lessons.

Personal account of Joyce Nesmith (1995)
Alexandria, Virginia

DANGER

*Charlie and Starbright reached the southern point of the beach
and turned back. The storm was getting stronger by the minute.
Now the stallion was racing against the wind. His nostrils flared.*

*Suddenly a burst of strength ripped through Starbright. He
raced across the sand as if he had wings. Violent, whipping
wings.*

*Charlie tugged on the reins with all her might, but she could
no longer hold the horse.*

*She dug her fingers into his whipping mane. For the first time
she was afraid.*

*Starbright made a flying leap over a piece of driftwood.
Charlie lost her grip and was flung in a high arc. She landed on
the sand, and lay there unconscious. The stallion never paused,
but galloped up into the dunes.*

Krista Ruepp, Midnight Rider

On a Kentucky breeding farm, a pasture full of Thoroughbred mares and foals is the equine equivalent of Tiffany's display window at the peak of the holiday season. Each horse represents a small fortune, and a gathering of them is easily worth a mint. Many of my young days were spent fondly gazing at the jewels of Hartland. At eight years old, the economic realities of the herd counted for little compared to the way my heart raced at the sight of horses running free.

On one memorable day, for reasons I still can't completely fathom, I found myself suddenly gripped by a conviction that the mares grazing so peaceably in the pasture were asking me to set them free. Conviction and action blended in an instant. With little thought of consequences, I jumped down from my fence rail and opened the gate.

It took the herd a few minutes to realize their opportunity. At first the horses merely continued grazing, nursing, and napping. Then one and now another swung a great head in the direction of the opening, back toward each other as if to confirm they were all seeing the same thing, then back toward the gate. I don't remember for sure, but it's quite possible I even called to them, encouraging them to leave. Certainly that would have been consistent with my wishes.

I must have shivered when they first stirred toward my invitation. An entire herd of horses in motion is a marvelous thing, and I would have been thrilled to have created such a marvel with my own hands and will. Then they were moving—at first walking, then trotting, and, finally, lifting their hooves into full flight, mares and foals alike, surging into the breech I had made.

My little brother Danny was about three at the time. He had trailed me to the pasture that day, as he often did. Focused as I was on the horses and their longing to be free, I gave him no thought as I watched wide-eyed from behind the gate, which I kept between the accelerating blur and me. It was not until the entire herd was rushing in my direction that I saw him, standing alone and inconceivably small, directly in the flight path of the stampede. Immobilized by shock, I clutched the rails of the gate as the horses bore down on him, then parted like runoff rushing around a boulder, before reuniting on the other side, leaving him untouched.

My relief was so immense that it took me several moments to realize Danny was safe but the horses were not. They were galloping down the driveway, flying headlong toward the massive stone entrance that opened onto a four-lane highway.

My father caught sight of the herd from a distance and gave one of his shrill whistles I always believed could be heard for miles. Yelling at a worker to get help, he jumped into his dark-green Chevy truck and raced to the entrance, matching his mechanical horsepower to the might of the horses. He barely beat them. A few men banded together in front of the oncoming wave of mares and foals, extending their arms and shouting *Whoa!* The racers veered off, circled around, and headed back up the long driveway. For a few minutes they galloped up and down the lengths of white post-and-board fencing, seeking another exit. When one of the lead mares finally was caught, the herd settled and submissively returned to their pasture under the watch of some very relieved workers and one extremely annoyed father.

I've often wondered why I freed the herd. Was it an expression of my fascination with the thrill of flight? Was I testing my independence or control or power? Did I act on the naive notion that all horses deserve to be free? Or was I perhaps rebelling against the confines that fenced my own life with horses—the financial constraints, the gender boundaries, the childhood limits? Maybe I just wanted to test whether I alone could will the herd into motion.

Whatever was running through my eight-year-old mind at the time, I look back on the event and recognize behind it an element that colors perhaps every relationship between a woman and a horse: danger and fear and the excitement that comes when the two are blended.

*U*nder the trees of the forest it was dark, but the air was clear, and the girl walked bravely along. She did not know much about trolls, only that they were dangerous and sometimes lived under bridges. She did not know which way through the forest her father had taken the boy. She walked ahead on the path, and when the path branched, she said to the toy horse she carried, "Which way?"

The horse was in her left hand, so its head pointed left, and she went that way.

She walked on and walked on. She saw nothing but the tall dark trees, and a few birds flitting silently, and here and there in the thin snow the tracks of mice and rabbits, foxes and deer.

Days are short in the dark winter of the North. The yellow sunlight slanted through the trees and then was gone. The light was cold and blue.

"Oh, horse," said the girl, "should we go back home?"

The wooden horse kept looking straight ahead.

The girl walked on. She felt lonely, so she talked to the wooden horse. "Mother can't look for my brother," she said. "The baby is delicate, and she has to stay with it. So we should find the trolls and bring my brother home. But where shall we spend the night?"

The wooden horse kept looking at the path ahead of them, so she went on. The air grew lighter as the path led out of the forest to the bank of the river. The open sky above the water was still bright with evening. But the river ran swift and dark, and across it was a narrow wooden bridge.

The girl was afraid. She took a step forward and then stood still. She took one more step, and one more, and now she stood on the bridge. And over the side of the bridge, from underneath it, a great, long arm came reaching, and a great, wide hand groped toward her.

She held the toy horse tight in her hand and held still, whispering, "Oh, horse! Help me!"

She felt the wooden toy move in her hand. It quivered, and trembled, and then it leapt from her hand. As its wooden feet struck the bridge, they turned to hooves, and it stood upon them, a real horse, full size, bright red, with a bridle and saddle of flowers, and bright, fiery eyes!

The horse stamped on the planks. The huge arm drew back, and a voice shouted from underneath the bridge, "Who's that stamping on my bridge?"

"Me! The red mare!"

Then the girl and the red mare listened, and they heard the troll under the bridge bumping and banging about and swearing and having a tantrum.

"It's afraid of me," the red mare said to the girl with a snort, and she stamped on the planks again.

"Stop that!" the troll yelled. "Go on! Go across! Go away!"

"Mount on my back," said the red mare to the girl, and quickly she mounted onto the flower saddle and took up the reins that were a leafy vine.

There on the red mare's back she had no fear.

Ursula K. Le Guin, *A Ride on the Red Mare's Back*

MYTHOLOGY AND LEGEND are filled with stories of horses carrying men and women to the heavens; they're also packed with tales of horses carrying humans to hell. The Greek sun god Helios guided "his four fiery steeds up the vault of the heavens" every day, but when his mortal son Phaethon tried the same feat, the younger man lost control of the chariot team and perished. The White Stallion who nudged Gretchen's old mare to take the lost girl home was a mythical hero of western American folklore, but the pale horse of the Bible signified death. Horses of fable have always galloped around the globe under devils as well as angels and as symbols of darkness as well as light. The animal's contradictory imagery is testimony to a timeless tension in humankind's relationship with the creatures: Horses can be dangerous; they may risk our very lives. Yet, despite the risks, horses can transport us to heights no other animal can.

Without the danger, the heights horses carry us to might not be possible. Drs. Adele von Rust McCormick and Marlena Deborah McCormick articulate what they call "the beneficial character of fear," contending that "periods of fear and anxiety are necessary components of personal growth." In my own riding and my work with other women riders, I have often observed that when horses expose us to a danger that we bring under control, we become stronger and self-confidence roots itself deeper in our souls. This may be one of the intrinsic allures of the horse for women: They give us a sense of danger that produces at least a momentary thrill and also rewards us with a lingering sense of our own strength as we ride our way out of peril.

The forces, the materials, the laws
Of all creation are balanced

On the course of that chariot and those horses.
A boy could not hope to control them.
You are my son, but mortal. No mortal
Could hope to manage those reins.
Not even the gods are allowed to touch them. . . .

Yes, even Jupiter
High god of all heaven, whose hand
Cradles the thunderbolt—
He keeps his fingers off those reins.
And who competes with him?

Our first stretch is almost vertical.
Fresh as they are, first thing,
It is all the horses can do to get up it.
Then on to mid-heaven. Terrifying
To look down through nothing
At earth and sea, so tiny.
My heart nearly struggles out of my body
As the chariot sways.
Then plunges towards evening—
There you need strength on the reins. . . .

But Phaethon, too drunk with his youth to listen,
Ignored the grieving god

And leapt aboard, and catching the reins
From his father's hands, joyfully thanked him.

Pyrois, Eous, Aethon, Phlegon—
The four winged horses stormed to be off.
Their whinnyings quaked the air-waves,

A writhing crackle of interference
Throughout heaven. . . .

The crazed horses scattered.
They tore free, with scraps of the yoke,
Trailing their broken reins.
The wreckage fell through space,
Shattered wheels gyrating far apart,
Shards of the car, the stripped axle,
Bits of harness—all in slow motion
Sprinkled through emptiness.

Phaethon, hair ablaze,
A fiery speck, lengthening a vapour trail,
Plunged towards the earth
Like a star
Falling and burning out on a clear night.

Ted Hughes, "Phaethon," from *Tales from Ovid*

IN MY LATE twenties, I met and fell in lust with an artistic stallion who brought danger as real as any runaway horse into my life.

Bret was an exceptionally handsome man and a seductive talker. He was a talented painter and interior designer, work that brought him to a gallery opening in Greenville, Delaware's historic horse country, where we met. Three months later he moved into the guesthouse I occupied on one of the town's great old estates. Bret's public polish masked a dark private side that included an addiction to drugs, and friends and family who lived on the border of the law. His territory was a world of temptation and abandon that I'd never dreamed of, much less visited. We spent a year and a half together. It is a time I view now as a long and hazardous ride on a wild mustang—thrilling at first but ultimately perilous.

Bret had a friend in Manhattan, an artist who lived in the loft of a vast warehouse across from one of the piers on the Hudson River. The New York art world glittered as a rich and unexplored universe on the evening Bret and I sped north from Delaware to spend a weekend night with Roy shortly after New Year's, and I was eager to view it from an insider's perspective. Bret and I caught up with our host at a chic restaurant near Central Park where he worked as a waiter, ordering drinks at the bar as we waited for his shift to end. When Roy finally joined us and a growing crowd of his lively friends, he became our own one-man show, regaling us all with his stories about his well-heeled clients, extravagant New Year's Eve parties, celebrity gossip, and new art projects. I'd never heard stories like these in Lexington or anywhere else, and I was enthralled.

Although it was already past midnight, I didn't hesitate when Roy proposed a prowl through Central Park and the streets of New York. By then the merry bunch had latched on to a magnum of champagne, and it passed from mouth to mouth as we wandered through the night. At one of the fountains in the park where the water had frozen into a piece of midwinter art, we stopped and pretended its Greek statues were coming to life to party with us. On the streets, we were hugely entertained by the way the night wanderers who huddled for warmth over steaming manholes seemed to vanish when they stepped back, leaving behind nothing but the vapor cloud where they'd stood. The effect was better than any illusionist's act. Roy was our trailblazer, and he was leading us through an enchanted forest full of sorcerers and beasties. I followed with eyes wide open and nostrils flared, a young mare with my own stallion at my side, as oblivious to impending danger as I'd been when I threw the gate open back at Hartland.

We ended up at Roy's place in the heart of night. His loft occupied a small section of a big open brick warehouse that was cold, damp, dark, and unforgettably rank. In the cavern of the building that was his living space and studio, he had arrayed his work: life-size plastic molds of humans with shrouds covering their bodies and statues of phalluses. I was tiring but the men were anxious for more. They finally left me behind for a couple of hours as they continued their revels. I was soon sorry I hadn't joined them. In the midst of Roy's art, I felt surrounded by death. When Bret and Roy returned and Roy wanted to show us the pier where he went for inspiration, I was even more reluctant to remain alone with the shrouds and penises than to venture onto the derelict waterfront. I followed the men back into the streets.

On the piers, the only sounds were boards creaking under our feet, the swish of unseen currents, and the echoes of Bret and Roy's laughter. When I looked toward my feet, I could see slats with gaps big enough to swallow me and drop me to the Hudson River far below. The few squatters we passed were mere bodies, broken people huddled into corners, foul with the smell of booze and vomit and desperation. I wanted to go home but Roy and Bret only laughed more boisterously. Drunk and on intimate terms with the underworld of their souls and the New York night, they were comfortable in this forbidding forest. I was not. I had found a boundary for my appetite for danger.

The sun was rising on the other side of the island by the time our threesome returned to the loft. A few hours later the *New York Times* arrived, carrying within its pages a small report that a violent murder had taken place on the piers the night before. The news item served as a punctuation mark, a period, that brought closure to an experience that would forever after inform my risk taking.

It wasn't long after my evening among the death molds and the winos of the waterfront that I broke up with my artist lover. I hadn't lost my appetite for excitement but I'd recognized the difference between mindless abandon and measured risk.

I found that the drive to be accepted, or rather not to be unaccepted, was being supplanted. . . . The mare's instinct for survival, latent within, had asserted itself to take care of me. I was ready at last to accept and accede it.

She has become a rather extraordinary rider, under the tutorship of a more than extraordinary teacher—B.B., which is her pet name for Buffalo Bill. She pronounces it beeby. He has not only taught her seventeen ways of breaking her neck, but twenty-two ways of avoiding it. He has infused into her the best and surest protection of a horseman—confidence. He did it gradually, systematically, little by little a step at a time, and each step made sure before the next was essayed. And so he inched her along up through terrors that had been discounted by training before she reached them, and therefore were not recognizable as terrors when she got to them. Well, she is a daring little rider now, and is perfect in what she knows of horsemanship. By and by she will know the art like a West Point cadet, and will exercise it as fearlessly. She doesn't know anything about sidesaddles. Does that distress you? And she is a fine performer, without any saddle at all. Does that discomfort you? Do not let it; she is not in any danger, I give you my word.

Mark Twain, *"A Horse's Tale"*

MANY YEARS AGO, during my "have-saddle-will-travel" horse-training days, I met a woman named Cheryl who loved to ride but was all but paralyzed by the danger of it. She was a middle-aged professional, ambitious yet soft and sweet. Her horse was a beautiful chestnut Thoroughbred who had seen and done much in life. He was eighteen, with scarred legs and padded hooves but generally a nice fellow.

During our first meeting, Cheryl confessed that she and her horse weren't working as partners and that he often scared her. She had taken lessons with many instructors but none of them had overcome the hurdle of her fright. She was almost to the point of giving up, yet the promise of enjoying her horse without fear kept her trying. She heard about me through a friend and thought she might as well give her riding one more chance with somebody new.

We met at the white wooden barn where her horse was stabled, and I watched as she put his saddle and bridle on. I noticed the severe bit and the addition of draw reins, which are training devices to be used only by the softest of expert hands. After she'd tacked up the horse, he and I set off for the arena with Cheryl following. When she joined us in the ring, my jaw dropped open. She had added two-inch spurs and was armed with a long dressage whip for each hand. Here was a woman who said she wanted to work with her horse as a partner yet she was decked out for battle. Her horse knew it; I could read his tension when he ground his teeth at her approach.

Cheryl said she needed all the gear "to make the horse go." From the start she'd been fearful on horseback, but she had ridden for a time without the artificial aids. When the horse, detecting her anxieties, began to behave badly—bolting and throwing her more than once—previous instructors had suggested the armament. Nobody had ever identified or addressed the fear that was the source of her troubles.

The arena was Cheryl's whole equestrian world; she dared not venture outside it on horseback. Though there were miles of beautiful trails and open fields surrounding the enclosed ring, she did not trust her horse or herself outside the gate. As we came to know each other over the following weeks and months, it turned out Cheryl felt overmatched in many parts of her life; riding only happened to be the most fearsome of them.

Within these limits, we began. We set up a twice-weekly schedule of lessons during which she was to wear no spurs or carry any whips. She was also always to wear a safety helmet. Ironically, this was the one protective device that could really make her safe, yet she'd never taken up the practice of wearing one. From then on, she would. In between lessons, I rode her horse with no force or expectations. During those sessions, I stretched and massaged him before mounting and I took him out on the trails beyond the ring. On the ground, I taught him to stretch and round his back and move forward—lessons intended to give him pleasure in his own movement and in training. As I jogged with him in hand and played with him, he began to watch my body language and tune in to a human partner in a new way. This horse had raced for many years, been a jumper, and now was a dressage horse. Both Cheryl and her horse had plenty of ability and desire; they simply had misplaced the cords of pleasure and cooperation that should have bound them together as a happy team.

After only two weeks, the terror I read on Cheryl's face during that initial lesson evolved first into occasional signs of enjoyment, then to a sense of relief, and finally to an expression of relaxation and confidence. Cheryl and I worked together for several months, and she slowly gained mastery over the exaggerated dangers of riding her horse.

As the horse changed and softened, so did Cheryl. With my gentle encouragement, she involved herself increasingly in all aspects of the horse's training, eventually working with him on the ground as well as in the saddle. She began to massage him every time she rode, and this made their bond even deeper. He began to go and slow and stop when asked, even in the absence of any punishing actions, and he stopped his frightening bolting stunts. We changed his bit to an inviting smooth snaffle, took away the restrictive draw reins, and adjusted his saddle and pad for a better fit. I borrowed another horse, and Cheryl and I even went out on some trail rides together, just talking and enjoying the countryside. In a few months Cheryl was a new rider and a changed woman. She was eager to ride and her horse was happy to carry her. A partnership was developing. She began to brag about her horse and to tell friends she was thinking about showing him. Cheryl confided that her situation at work was improving. She decided to lose some weight and buy new clothes. She was testing her wings not only on her horse but also throughout her life.

When we met, Cheryl had grasped the concept of controlling danger but she had sought control with external devices that only heightened the tension and fear both she and the horse were feeling about their encounters. More than technical riding instruction, she had needed to find her own inner courage. The old compression and restriction in her body and the horse's body had made danger imminent for her. Once relaxed on her horse and within herself, she was at last safe and comfortable. Her emerging partnership with her horse carried this rider to a new place of inner confidence, a place that was all hers to grow or rein in and where no instructor, trainer, friend, or business associate could ever have taken her. Overriding her fears, Cheryl entered another world.

People can and do get hurt on and around horses, and the injuries can be grave. The fact that we so consistently seek out these creatures despite the risks is testimony to both their magnetism and the strength of our desire for mastery over our fears. One of the gifts a horse offers us is a chance to explore constructive ways to meet danger and manage our private terrors.

Freida is a woman in her fifties who has always lived a sheltered, single life. She is intelligent but timid, a woman constantly worrying aloud about something. When I'm around Freida, most of what she talks about are her fears. Yet even though she is not a natural athlete or even particularly fit, she regularly competes in riding events that daunt horsewomen half her age and twice her ability. On a regular basis, she puts herself at risk and then refuses to be cowed by it. She rides an old and temperamentally predictable gelding. He is one of the constructive ways she manages danger to herself. In him, she has found a partner whom she trusts and can rely upon to take care of her and make her feel safe, important, and empowered. He brings to her awards and honors she may not receive in any other area of her life; he draws out her hidden abilities and calms her fears of inadequacy and disconnection. With such a stabilizing partner, she is able to manage and control danger. The reward is a feeling of personal and social acceptance and a sense of accomplishment.

But she goes beyond choosing the right mount. She

prepares herself and her horse thoroughly for every event. She confesses she hardly sleeps during an event weekend because her mind and emotions are so busy analyzing every potential pitfall.

None of these measures eliminates the dangers of eventing, and Freida is still afraid. But when the signal comes to start, she is able to perform successfully. Her fears are virtually never realized. She triumphs over the danger. I like to think that, for all the worrying she does about riding and eventing and every detail of her life, it's just a fraction of what she'd do if she weren't routinely seeking and surviving risk as a horsewoman. Fret though she might, she doesn't need spurs and whips to overcome the dangers of riding hard because she's found a way to master her fears from within. It may even be that her incessant verbalizing gives her a measure of organization and control over her fears. By the time she actually has to confront the dangers, she's literally talked them to death.

I felt that I must go back and live and die in Waimanu rather than descend that scathed steep, and being stupid with terror flung myself from my horse, forgetting that it was much safer to trust to his four feet than to my two, and to an animal without "nerves," dizziness, or "the foreknowledge of death," than to my palsied, cowardly self.
Isabella Bird, *Six Months in the Sandwich Islands*

EVERY TIME MY mare Theo and I clear a jump, I'm more confident about the next one. The same holds true for a woman confronting any hurdle. We all encounter barriers and obstacles, many of them dangerous and all of them capable of arousing fear. Whether our "jumps" come on a cross-country obstacle course or within our work-places and homes or simply rise from the landscapes of our own hearts the way Freida's do, we gain confidence every time we soar over them. Danger and our mastery of it become moments that make us more capable of handling the next danger and facing other risks.

In Ursula K. Le Guin's modern fable, the little girl and the red mare ride together to the High House where the trolls live with all their snarling troll children. The mare concocts a daring plan to lure the trolls from their cave while the girl sneaks inside to find and bring out the brother that the trolls have stolen.

Then the mare reared up on her hind legs and let out a great ringing neigh and came down stamping on her forehooves. "Trolls!"

There was a sound of roaring and yelling inside the mountain. Trolls came pouring out of the door, dozens and scores of them, hairy and scaly and scowling, and, oh, they were ugly trolls. Their arms were long and their hands were wide; their skins were white and their eyes small. They came running out so fast, reaching for the red mare's reins, that she barely leapt away in time. She galloped up into the rocks and snow and darkness of the mountainside. Some of the trolls carried flaring torches, and all of them went running after her, shouting, "Catch her! Head her off! Catch her reins! Drive her to the cliff's edge!"

Ursula K. Le Guin, *A Ride on the Red Mare's Back*

THE GIRL WITNESSES what can only be a waking nightmare in the murderous tide of trolls. Literally and metaphorically, the horse has led her to the doorstep of her worst fears. But the mare's plan works. The girl finds her brother amid the riotous troll children, and, after brief resistance from him ("I like it here. I can do anything I like here"), she carries him out of the cave. Just as a troll is about to plunge a knife into the mare, the sun's first ray falls on the calamitous scene. The trolls are transformed into a circle of stones ringing a chipped and somewhat battered toy wooden horse. The children set off for home, the toy in hand. When they reach the bridge where the mare had sprung to life, the boy is frightened.

> "*Oh,*" *cried the little boy,* "*this is where the trolls came and took me from my father!*"
>
> *He did not want to set foot on the planks of the bridge, but his sister held his hand and said,* "*Come on. Don't be afraid. This troll is our friend now.*"
>
> Ursula K. Le Guin, *A Ride on the Red Mare's Back*

THE HORSE HAD carried the girl into danger, as it may carry any of us, but her triumph conquered her fears and gave her courage for the new challenges that lay ahead.

POWER

It was a grand race. The whole post was there, and there was such another whooping and shouting when the seventeen kids came flying down the turf and sailing over the . . . hurdles—oh, beautiful to see! Halfway down, it was kind of neck and neck, and anybody's race and nobody's. Then, what should happen but a cow steps out and puts her head down to munch grass, with her broadside to the battalion, and they a-coming like the wind; they split apart to flank her, but she?—why, she drove the spurs home and soared over that cow like a bird! and on she went, and cleared the last hurdle solitary and alone. . . .

Mark Twain, "A Horse's Tale"

*B*ecause they lived just down the block, I often spent the night with my grandparents after we moved from Hartland. It was very late on one of these nights—or, at least, it seemed very late on my child's inner clock—when the phone rang with a message that carried me to one of my early lessons in horsepower.

It was a groom from Alsab Farm where my PaPa was an adviser to the racehorse breeding operation and where a hot new stallion had just arrived to stand, the proper terminology for being put to stud. Somehow the horse had escaped his handler and was running loose. The workers were in full panic. Drawn from bed by the ringing telephone and the sudden electricity in the air, I listened to my grandfather's side of the conversation, wide awake with excitement and hope.

Hanging up the phone, PaPa reached for his gray flannel fedora and headed for the door in a single fluid motion, but he wasn't fast enough to evade me. If the stallion was loose, I wanted to be there when he was captured. I begged PaPa to take me, promising everything within my nine-year-old powers if he would allow me to come along. He was understandably reluctant. A loosed stallion, wild in the night, is a danger to anybody in its path, and I was a small anybody in my flannel nightgown and bare feet. Somehow, in spite of the risks, I needled from him a reluctant "Yes."

Pinto is out again! He kicks his door
Till the bolts give. Last time he only wandered
To the trough to gulp the freezing water
Then back into his stall. But now he bursts
Bristling to the cold, bright black and white
Through all of us, across the radiant yard.
The stablegirls run shouting. . . .

Pinto is out! The boy sent to pile snow
Across their road, warning of six foot drifts
In the next hollow, looks up—hurls a spade
As Pinto wheels, straight through the open gate
Across the unwalked white which was the field.

> Alison Brackenbury, from "Breaking Out"
> in *The Poetry of Horses*

I DIDN'T GIVE him a chance to rethink his decision. Grabbing a coat and my scuffed penny loafers, I dashed to the car and slid onto the red leather front seat of his '57 Chevy. As we sped through the darkness and turned onto Todds Road toward the barn, I breathed the intoxicating smells of the night air and the scents of my grandfather's world. The Chevy smelled of a power that had nothing to do with what was under the hood but that forever is linked in my mind with horses.

Approaching the farm, we spotted the stallion a few hundred yards away, his eyes flashing in the wash of our headlights. Drunk on his freedom, the steed rushed across the landscape like night itself—tossing his head, pawing the ground, sweat and foam leaving long white streaks on his gleaming coat. PaPa assessed the situation and decided it would be better to drive the horse into the barn than try to corner him in a paddock. He left me in the car briefly while conferring with his grooms, then returned to order me into the barn, where I was told to press myself against the wall and remain until the horse was maneuvered inside and brought under control.

"Don't move," he ordered as soon as I was situated. Then he was gone, and I was alone in the dark.

Outside, I could hear the cries of the grooms and the roar of my grandfather as the men stumbled over the ground trying to direct the great rebellious horse. If my grandfather's plan was sound, I knew that at any second, the quiet inside the barn would be shattered by the thunder of the stallion's hooves, the shriek of his protests, the clamor of the men trying to capture him. The bug lights over the center aisle glowed green with the night cold, and the vapor of my breath escaped in short, excited bursts.

And then he was there—eyes rolling, nostrils flaring and snorting, his entire body puffed up in fury and independence and manliness, a dragon of a horse who poured smoke from his nose and breathed steam through his skin. Never had I been so close to anything so large, so powerful, so full of energy, so dangerous. He was terrifying and life threatening and magnificent, all at the same time, and I felt I had crossed some invisible border into a world beyond myself merely by being in his presence.

He paws fiercely, rejoicing in his strength, and charges into the fray. He laughs at fear, afraid of nothing; he does not shy away from the sword. The quiver rattles against his side, along with the flashing spear and lance. In frenzied excitement he eats up the ground; he cannot stand still when the trumpet sounds. At the blast of the trumpet he snorts, "Aha!" He catches the scent of battle from afar, the shout of commanders and the battle cry.

Job 39: 21–25 (New International Version)

HURRIEDLY THE GROOMS closed the door at one end of the barn and then at the other. The runaway was trapped. We were trapped. Over their shouted directions to one another and the horse and the clatter of hooves striking the hard floor, I heard the rumble of my own heart, rearing and spinning with the glorious omnipotent creature.

Compared with the slow motion of anticipation, the finale was brief. Realizing he was cornered, the young stud soon gave up his revolt and allowed a lead rope to be looped around his neck and the leather halter carefully slipped onto his head. The grooms led the stallion into his stall and began rubbing him with wisps of crisp straw to dry his coat. As I watched from the stall door, PaPa ran his hands around the horse's body to make sure there were no wounds or bruises. He told the stable hands to wrap the horse's strong legs in standing-support bandages made of white linen and cotton and to secure them with large safety pins. The grooms offered water in small doses and placed a few flakes of sweet hay in the horse's manger. The stallion was tired. When the light outside his stall was extinguished, he was content to munch and rest.

Quiet regained the upper hand, and my grandfather led me through the darkness first to the car and then home to bed. I must have been exhausted, but I imagine that I lay awake the whole night replaying and reliving the memory, recalling the sensation of the stallion's unleashed power pulsing through my veins and filling me with a wild desire to run through the night.

. . . Come, let me taste my horse,
Who is to bear me like a thunderbolt.

William Shakespeare, *Henry IV, Part I*
(Act IV, scene i)

IT IS NO accident that "horsepower" is the Western world's standard measure of power. A scientist will tell us that one horsepower is equal to 745.7 watts of energy—33,000 foot-pounds of brute force—per minute. When machines first supplanted horses as the work engines of society, they often took their names from the equine vocabulary. Before the days of iron and steel, ships were sometimes called wooden horses. When trains replaced the horse-drawn vehicle for long-distance travel, they were known as iron horses, and when ferryboats came into use, the Indians could find no better metaphor for them than "the horses that walk on water."

Women are drawn to the power of horses. On an earth where most of us are shorter, smaller, and less muscular than most members of the opposite sex—where "manpower" is the standard measure of human force, not "womanpower"—horses are the great equalizer. No man on foot is a match for a woman on horseback, and any woman on horseback is a match for any man similarly mounted.

A woman doesn't need a scientist to tell her about a horse's power; she feels it in her bones and her muscles and her heart. Whether she rides a Thoroughbred racehorse or a backyard saddle pony, whether she jumps competitively or walks local trails or merely circles the ring at a stable, a woman on horseback is bigger, stronger, and faster than she is on foot, and those qualities increase and empower her.

I know a woman in nearby Fort Collins who grew up in a big city and only saw horses on television when she was young. As an adult, Linda spent a couple of vacations at dude ranches, where the main attraction for her was the riding. Even as a beginner, she found the power of the horse addictive. "There's nothing else I know that gives me the same sense of being on top of the world," she says. I share that sense. One of my lasting Hartland memories is of the day that turf writer and racing socialite Jobie Arnold lifted me onto her 17-hand Thoroughbred hunter, Handaul. I can still remember thinking that if I could walk this giant around the ring, I was ready for anything. My Theo is also on the tall side—16.2 hands from the ground to her withers, a bit over my full height of five feet four inches. Nearly forty years after my brief ride on Handaul, I must admit that the allure of a tall horse still moves me. One of the things I love about Theo is the sensation I experience of being boosted into the skies.

What delight
To back the living steed that challenges
The wind for speed!—seems native more of air
Than earth!—whose burden only lends him fire!—
Whose soul in his task, turns labour into sport!

Who makes your pastime his! I sit him now!
He takes away my breath!—He makes me reel!
I touch not earth—I see not—hear not—all
Is ecstasy of motion!

James Sheridan Knowles, *The Love Chase*
(Act II, scene iii)

A WOMAN NEED not own or lease or ride a horse to claim its might. In times of threat or sadness or fear or failure, simply culling through my past experiences with horses and reliving chosen moments can give me strength in a moment of need. Some of these memories are as new as this morning, and others, like one I have saved from an early riding lesson, are quite old. What I claim from the riding-lesson memory is the moment I fell off an extremely tall horse I was riding and everything went black. When I came around, I was breathless and a bit unnerved. The teacher allowed me a brief time-out, then ordered me back into the saddle. I was reluctant, but I obeyed the directions and moved through the rest of that lesson and the following ones successfully. This is only one of the memories I claim when I feel fearful or intimidated. Recalling powerful moments such as these infuses me with a sense of my own strength.

There are women who take strength from merely looking at the image of a horse in a photograph or a painting or a sculpture or by reading about horses or watching them. I remember asking my grandfather to save his horse magazines for me. Once a stack was mine, I would hungrily turn the pages for hours looking for dream horses to complete my imaginary stable. I have known other young girls who drew nothing but horses, filling sheet after sheet of paper with dun and spotted and bay ponies as if mere repetition might bring the horses to life or link horse spirits to their own emerging feminine souls. When I see the Budweiser Clydesdales pulling a wagon through the snow on television, I am reminded of the times I have driven a team of draft horses and felt the exhilaration of controlling horses of such immense size and magnificence.

She had piles of drawing-books which she showed me, full of drawings, paintings in watercolors, technicolored in crayons of horses of all manners and kinds and patterns and positions and movements. And what was interesting to me was the fact that in not one of these books was there a drawing of a horse as we see them in the world. They were all of horses as they walk only in the light between dreaming and waking or, as I would have thought of it, that light which presided over my portion of the great memory of the world of gods and titans of Greece.

Yet later as I went with her and her husband to some of her sporting events, not only in Spain but in France and Switzerland, she was dressed as impeccably as any other feminine rider in the field, and no one would have known that the horse she was riding and the race she was trying to win was not of the then and there, but of her own special within and forever.

Sir Laurens van der Post, *About Blady: A Pattern Out of Time*

WHETHER WE RIDE them or draw them, whether we are young in our relationship with them or mature, horses offer us an endless opportunity to feel accomplished. Putting on a horse show as a child and winning my pretend "class" as a girl-horse gave me a sense of confidence in myself. Later, when I fell off a lesson horse and got back on, I experienced the tumble as a step forward, not a defeat. I still remember how high I held my chin when I finally competed in my first real horse show when I was twelve at the Scott County Fair and took home a ribbon. Even more than the prize, those moments brought me the dizzying sensations of pride and joy, exposed me to the sweet taste of success and acceptance beyond my small circle of family and friends.

Especially as an emerging teenager but much later—all the way until today—those accomplishments collected in my heart as a savings account of power I could draw upon at lower moments.

A woman can build her own account at any level of horsemanship. Learning to mount and "sit the horse" is enough for many people to feel good. After all, riding is risky; conquering a perfectly natural hesitation to sit on an animal so tall and fast and with a mind of its own is an achievement. Once comfortable being with a horse, most of us find ourselves wanting to move to the next level. We start learning to move with the horse and feel his rhythm. When we do, we chalk up another personal best and make a deposit for future withdrawal. With horses, positive results are immediate and infinite. Courage begins to grow in our hearts, forging new independence and mettle. We feel confident enough to share the news of our budding skill with friends. Some of us go so far as to boast about being told we looked pretty good up there. After all, no matter how we look, walk, talk on our own, we can all look good on a horse.

As drawing does, merely handling horses can give us a sense of triumph and power. I enjoy having my mare Theo well turned out. This horse-show term indicates a horse is well groomed and conditioned. The mare's shiny, bright appearance of happiness and health is evidence that I have skill and expertise. It is because of my good care and attention to her looks, her manners, and her attitude that she is impressive in public. Her beauty and refinement reinforce my sense of dignity and ability.

The women seemed perfectly at home in their gay, brass-bossed, high peaked saddles, flying along astride, bare-footed, with their orange and scarlet riding dresses streaming on each side beyond their horses' tails, a bright kaleidoscopic flash of bright eyes, white teeth, shining hair, garlands of flowers and many colored dresses.

Isabella Bird, *Six Months in the Sandwich Islands*

RIDING AND REMEMBERING riding give me a sense of power that I carry with me, but horses also strengthen me by teaching me the power of passion.

Most horses have passion bred into them. My Theo was bred for speed, and that's given her a passion to run. Almost nothing puts her into such a contented mood as a good, hard gallop. Other horses are bred for other passions. Quarter Horses often possess it for cutting cattle. Paso Finos—literally, fine walkers—have it for their gait. Some horses have a passion to show off. A Saddlebred in his stall is simply a horse among horses; give him an admiring audience and you'd think there was an extra-large carrot waiting for the horse with the highest head and fanciest trot.

Horses take their passions and their power for granted in ways that few of us humans ever manage. They are profoundly intuitive, and they trust their intuitiveness. Theo was born to run, so she seeks opportunities to run. When she runs well, she is fulfilled. Intuition tends to be suspect as a source of direction among humans, but I believe most of us are like Theo and the cutting horses and the Paso Finos: We derive personal power from exercising the gifts that are the most instinctive.

When I appear before groups of women and talk to them about power, I always advise them to search out their passion. By identifying and using passion to guide and drive you through each and every day, you gain personal power and freedom. It is like an inner fire that ignites every time you connect to your passion. I was lucky; I found mine early and enjoyed many opportunities to develop it. For most of the people who attend my clinics, they are as passionate about horses as I am. I have found that I receive a tremendous amount of energy from my love for horses that helps me in all of the other areas of my life. The fact that I feel so strongly about something refuels me when I need it. I gain power to make decisions, to move through a challenge and enjoy a sense of personal freedom. Not every woman is so fortunate. Yet all of us cherish in our hearts one, two, or several things that give us pleasure to perform, study, or merely think about. When we find something that excites or thrills us, even something that simply takes us to a soothing place, we have found the thread of a passion. Follow it! An Arabian mare doesn't need to ask herself what she's good at; the memory of it is carried in her hooves and her legs and her haunches, which are bred to carry her long distances over the desert sands.

We can and need to ask ourselves: *What are we good at? What do we enjoy? What kind of environment do we feel most comfortable in? What makes us feel most comfortable within ourselves? What in life makes us sparkle?*

We need to trust our intuitiveness to reveal our passions. In our passions we will find our power.

Well mounted on a strong, spirited horse—with a wide country before her—on a clear, cool day—with a love for all the beauty around her, of the noble animal beneath her, and glowing with the bounding life within her, a lady capable of enjoyment is certainly prepared for it then. The first gentle pace of the horse starts the warm blood in her veins, and as both become excited, the glow tingles to the very finger-tips. The close-clinging to the horse, the slight reliance upon stirrup and bit, and the generally light proportion of rider to steed, give a feeling of being possessed of the powers of a new life, of riding upon the whirlwind, and yet controlling it with a word.

"Ladies' Riding," *Hints to Horsekeepers:
A Complete Manual for Horsemen*

HORSES ARE EXPENSIVE to acquire, house, feed, and maintain so it's not surprising that when women talk about their passion for horses, it doesn't take long for the conversation to arrive at money. Few things come between a woman and a love of horseflesh quite as decisively as a shortage of funds. Certainly when I talk about my life with horses, the presence or absence of money has always been a part of the story. Even so, it saddens me when a woman says, "I'd love to ride, but I can't afford a horse." I want to say "Find a way to ride without affording one!"

For most of my life, I could not afford to keep a horse of my own. To exercise my passion, I borrowed or begged mounts, or traded out my labor for the hours I spent at their sides or on their backs. Of the four horses I have owned, I bought only one. The others were given to me, typically because they had behavioral problems that made them hard to sell. They were throwaways, and I was the grateful beneficiary of their bad habits.

Other women find other creative ways to be near horses. I think of Carrie Lynn, a Denver manicurist with a passion for riding that goes back to her childhood. Now in her mid-thirties and single, Carrie Lynn is focused on saving money to buy a home of her own. Owning a horse is definitely not in the savings plan. Yet she rides at least once a week and sometimes more. She's found a couple several miles from her home who own three horses. Because they can exercise only two of the animals at once, they are grateful to have Carrie Lynn ride the third. She is grateful to be riding for free. Riding feeds her soul and makes her feel alive in ways that nothing else does. Carrie Lynn doesn't need money to nurture her passion; she needs only resourcefulness and a commitment to caring about herself.

Our passions are rooted in our hearts and souls. Whether we recognize them at a young age or discover them along the way, they are a source of joy. Only after they take shape do we sometimes find there are barriers to exercising them. With horses, money can be a large one. I like to think of these obstructions to my passion as fallen trees or flooded streams on a course that only make me feel stronger when I fly over them.

In the preautomotive white culture of the West, the lack of a horse was the most telling giveaway that a man was poor. It was socially and economically defining, a determinant of acceptance or rejection. Among the Navajo and Apache, the number of horses a bridegroom paid for his bride was the prime indicator of her virtue and social standing. The horse-based economy is long gone in twenty-first-century America, but horses still connote money and money still implies a kind of power. This can be confusing. The power I wish for myself and every woman is a horse's power: the strength and peace and fulfillment that come from having a passion and from exercising it. Our society puts a premium on other forms of power: dominance, wealth, and status. In Kentucky where I was reared, the trio of wealth, power, and horses were forged into a seamless golden trinity that implied superiority.

While I was learning to overcome obstacles that separated me from my dreams of a life among horses, I was called upon from time to time to choose between the interior natural power of the horse and the exterior manufactured power of society. I remember in particular one wealthy racehorse owner who asked me to assess his stables and horse business. He insisted we discuss my findings in his luxury penthouse suite at a deluxe Lexington hotel, where he revealed after a long dinner that his real intent was to enlist me as his mistress.

"I will give you any horse you want and as many as you want, an unlimited wardrobe, jewels, and a healthy annual salary to conduct my horse business around the world." He smiled greasily. "All you have to do is be available to me at all times."

The horse world is a cottage industry and largely masculine. Cracking the wine bottle over his head might have been immensely satisfying, but it would have set up new barriers between myself and the horses I loved. I settled for telling him I was flattered but not available. Both statements were true. I'd spent too many years as a scrawny fence-sitter not to appreciate the worldly power and benefits this horseman's money could buy me, but I'd lived long enough as an independent woman to recognize their cost.

The horseman took my rejection with grace, but as we were waiting for the elevator, he turned and asked, "What kind of car are you driving?"

"A Datsun," I told him.

He snorted. "You can go tomorrow and pick out any car you want if you come to work for me."

As the elevator doors closed on him, I briefly imagined the car I might have picked out in the morning and the horses I might have owned. The shimmer of the man's wealth and power still mildly dazzled me, but what struck me even more was the sense of my own strength. In the end, my client's power extended only as far as his pocketbook could reach. Mine knew no limits. Nobody could own me but myself. Driving away in my Datsun, it was my PaPa's '57 Chevy I breathed. *This*, I thought with a sense of jubilation, *this* is horsepower.

GRAMBS ARONSON
AND THE WHITE PONY

Grambs Aronson was born in 1916, the child of American ex-patriates living in China. For most of her childhood, she suffered from tuberculosis of the hip. As a young child, her years were spent in bed with traction, casts, and splints. Once she was sufficiently recovered to venture out, she immersed herself in capturing the world she came to so late in pen-and-ink drawings.

One day in her early teens, Grambs ventured to a nearby stable she had heard about and met the Russian colonel who owned it. She had friends who rode at the colonel's stable and she had been enthralled by their stories. She knew her mother would forbid her to ride if she asked so she didn't ask. Colonel Bendersky, recognizing both the longing and the disability, said he believed she could ride safely and comfortably in an ornate sidesaddle in his possession. It would fit a pony named Masha, which is Mary in Russian.

The colonel had found Masha at the local racetrack where they raced Mongolian ponies. The mare was too big to race, and the colonel bought her and took her home. She got even bigger and foaled a beautiful white colt. He trained Masha to obey by voice command, which he delivered with a charming flair. If the mare heard "T-r-r-r-r-rot!" she would trot, or "Gall-O-O-O-O-p!" and she would gallop. If a handkerchief dropped to the ground in front of her, she stopped in her tracks. She was the perfect mount for Grambs's healing body.

At first, the stable master only allowed Grambs to ride Masha in the ring. Later he permitted her to go off into the countryside on her own. The pony gave Grambs a sense of freedom she had never known in her brief, confined life. It was only long after she began flying over the Chinese countryside regularly that she confessed her adventures to her mother, who reluctantly gave permission for the outings to continue.

Grambs often rode Masha into the local village, where she drew stares as a small white girl mounted on a white pony with an ornately decorated sidesaddle. It was hard for a sickly child from a foreign land to find a place for herself, but Masha was a consolation. Secure in her sidesaddle, Grambs felt she could roam the countryside with a confidante and best friend.

When Grambs left China at eighteen to attend art school in New York City on a scholarship, she said goodbye to Masha. By then, her countless hours on the pony's back had given the young woman a deep sense of her own strength and health. She took her sidesaddle with her, packing it in her steamer trunk. She knew she'd have no chance to ride in the new city life that awaited her, but the saddle was a totem she could touch to reclaim the power Masha taught her flying over the dry plains of what was then Tien-Tsin and now is Tian Jin.

Interview with Grambs Aronson,
New York City, New York

NURTURANCE

Throughout the few weeks of his life he could not remember a moment when his dam had not been beside him or at least within call. The first thing he saw when he woke from slumber was the sheltering body of his mother; it was the last thing he saw before falling asleep. He knew that he could rest in safety because his mother would never forsake him. But now she had gone. He had drawn back with a shudder of fear from her still form; he had been led, struggling, away from it by a soft-voiced human whose compassion he felt but could not understand.

Helen Griffiths, Horse in the Clouds

*H*orses possess an instinct to nurture themselves. A grazing horse is a horse taking care of herself in the most primal of ways. Her head is down, her munching is rhythmic, her ears flop lazily forward and back. Her tail swishes from time to time as she soaks the sunshine into her coat. She seeks out grasses, weeds, and herbs that feed her body and sense of wellness. Perhaps she wanders to water and sucks the coolness down the length of her neck. She finds the perfect dusty spot and lies down, getting a back rub as she rolls over to coat herself with natural defenses against bugs and the elements.

Horses instinctually enact all the nuances contained in the word "nurture." As a matter of habit, they feed, protect, sustain, support, train, and condition themselves every single day. Over thousands of years of neglect, we humans have been losing our instinct to nurture ourselves in the innate, self-satisfying way the grazing horse does. Too often we do only what we absolutely must to survive, and we do it with little pleasure or thoughtfulness. A relative, friend, coworker, neighbor, or even someone we see often in passing who makes us feel good just by recognizing us with a hello can help rekindle the feeling, but internally we have to do it for ourselves. Nurturance is acceptance; self-nurturance is self-acceptance.

My mother was my first nurturer and remains an irreplaceable one. She has fed me from earliest memory in countless ways. Before we moved to Hartland, my family lived in a cracker-box house on Preston Court in the small town of Versailles (pronounced ver-SALES by Kentuckians), where I could only dream of ponies and horses. Though she was never a horse person herself, my mother read the passion for horses in my heart and consistently found ways of nurturing it even in the absence of funds to provide me with the real thing.

One of the earliest gifts of nurturance I remember was a day when I was perhaps five years old. Mom showed me an old broom and told me this was to be my new horse. Together we would bring him to life. How excited I was! We went through my dad's sock drawer and found a beige sock that had lost its partner. From her button box, Mom selected eyes. We visited the local five-and-dime store, Ben Franklin's, and found felt and yarn for the horse's blaze, ears, and mane. Then we set to work. Into the sock went crumpled old newspaper to form an oblong head. Out came needles, thread, and glue to attach the eyes, stitch a mouth, give the fellow a respectable mane. When the horse's head was complete and tacked up with a shoestring bridle, she attached it to the broomstick with the straws of the broom trailing as the tail.

I watched a TV show every Wednesday afternoon called

Wendy Wonderful, a program about a puppet horse named Wendy and his best friend Mary Ann, the woman who hosted the show. In horsy Kentucky, this was the bluegrass country's answer to Shari Lewis and Lambchop, and I never missed it. Local children appeared on the show, where they asked Wendy questions. Mary Ann and Wendy conversed and usually came up with a humorous answer. Knowing how I doted on Wendy, Mom suggested I call my new horse Wendy Wonderful. Her suggestion was the finishing touch on the fantasy world that she had constructed for her girl-horse daughter, and it was one where I could ride every day.

I took the completed Wendy outside and threw my leg over the long handle of his back, taking the reins and squeezing my legs together to hold my mount securely. Lacking a riding helmet, I sported a cowboy hat that knotted under my chin and galloped Wendy up and down our cul de sac showing all our neighbors my new horse. Wendy was a great friend, a spirited mustang, and we were terrific partners until I wore him out with my cantering around our backyard, down the sidewalks, and up the walkways to knock on my friends' doors.

As I grew older, my mother continued to seek ways to nurture my passion for horses. She worked longer hours to pay for riding lessons, a hunt cap, and rubber riding boots and spent countless hours taxiing me to lesson stables where she waited at ringside as I reined real-life Wendys through fundamental exercises. When my first two years in college proved to be a waste of my time and my parents' money—I took subjects in which I had little native skill or interest and concentrated most of my energy on partying, at which I excelled—she was the one who found a fruitful escape route for me. Mom may have the manners of a pampered Southern belle, but she is pragmatic to the core. She said a woman needs to be able to take care of herself, and she figured I could best do that with horses. After I dropped out following my sophomore year, Mom called upon her father-in-law, my PaPa, and lobbied him to finance my training for the Horsemaster's certification course at the Potomac Horse Center. We knew no one else well enough to ask for help with the costly training, and she was determined I would have it. The alpha horse in her won his sponsorship.

I think of my mother as the first of my horse angels, one in a long line of women who have led me to horses and nourished my passion for them. Without exception, these are alpha mares whose wisdom made them natural leaders.

Peggy Cummings is a perfect example. We met when I was putting together my first Women & Horses Conference back in 1991. A horsewoman friend suggested her as a possible speaker and sent me some information about her. I was startled reading the material to find Peggy talking about riding in a way I didn't recognize. Even though we both went through similar training and received our Horsemaster's certification from the Potomac Horse Center, hers was a gentler language than I'd heard before. I couldn't even clearly imagine how she put her soft ideas like "floating" and "stretchy elbows" to work, but I was curious. I invited her to speak.

Peggy said she would have to attend the conference as an onlooker before she could commit to being a speaker. It was an unusual request but I agreed, assigned her a complimentary booth space, and looked forward to a face-to-face meeting with this intriguing woman.

In all, she was a lead horse. Not the dull silver metal, lead. But the LEED.

Diane Glancy, *"Lead Horse"*

WE MET IN New Brunswick, New Jersey, in the Cook's College auditorium before the first speaker took the stage. Peggy turned out to be a tall, solid woman in her mid-forties with an aura of infinite wisdom. She had something of a lumber in her walk yet she conveyed nothing but complete ease as she moved about her equipment, unpacking saddles and ropes and the skeleton model she used to illustrate rider body positions. She handled her tools as if they were extensions of her own hands. Part of me wanted to stay in her booth and do nothing but watch her move.

It was a long day for both of us, but we spent a few minutes at the end exchanging impressions. Peggy expressed admiration for my concept of giving the female rider information and equipment specific to her riding issues and gender, but she still wasn't ready to commit to a more visible presence in my public work. "I need to see you with your horse before I can consider working with you in the conferences or in any other way." We set up a time when she could meet with me and Diva, the mare I owned then, in Virginia.

The first time Peggy visited us, she watched me handle Diva in the stall, groom her, and tack her up. "Just do your normal routine and I'll be here," she said. It was an uncommon teaching strategy. Most instructors tend to show up, meet the student, and start issuing commands.

Diva and I were both going through a period of physical stress at the time. When I began to work with the mare in the arena, the horse was reasonably cooperative but clearly irritable and cranky. I wasn't much better myself. I could ride well only in one direction because my left hip and leg were stiff and wouldn't take orders from my mind. What's more, I'd suffered a rotator cuff tear that was only diagnosed shortly after my first meeting with Peggy; this further hampered my movement. It felt as if my body had disengaged itself from my heart and mind. I longed for the comfort and ability I had known in the saddle for more than three decades, but no matter how hard I focused on the task, I was failing. The harder I tried, the more I hurt from the inside all the way out.

Peggy could read my frustration. Eventually she asked if she could ride the horse. Before stepping into the stirrups, she loosened the girth and adjusted the saddle pad and saddle to find its level position. She placed thin, wedge-shaped sponges called shims under the saddle to help balance it on the mare's back, explaining that saddle position might be affecting my body and putting pressure in the wrong places for both the horse and me. Once she mounted and walked around for a few minutes, the horse clearly began to relax.

We weren't far into the session before the details of the physical trials Diva and I were both suffering worked their way to the surface. Peggy didn't dismiss any of them or demand that I change anything. She asked probing questions that demonstrated her attentiveness and made observations about how my discomforts might be affecting my riding. Leading me away from Diva, she placed her hand on my lower back as we walked together. Peg suggested I think of my body as a buoy on the water and focus on how the buoy rides the waves yet remains in balance. How the spine should align itself and how it affects the skeletal hinges at the hips, knees, and ankles was the point of her teaching that day.

Despite my lifetime on and around horses, Peggy's lessons were unlike any instruction I'd ever received. They went beyond mere technique to touch the neglected feminine spirit within. Peggy had studied Eastern and Western body awareness methodologies and blended them with her experience as an instructor to produce a riding system all her own. Because her techniques did not derive from the military, the hunt field, or the cowboy—as most of our riding traditions do—they were foreign and suspect in the mainstream horse world. But the mainstream horse world wasn't much on my mind that morning. I just wanted to work better with my horse, and Peggy was already making a lot of sense.

I remounted and rode Diva again, this time with Peggy matching our steps on the ground to foster my sense of balance and body awareness. "Close your eyes and feel every sensation the horse creates within you," she urged. "Remember the buoy." Already, I was moving my left leg again and Diva was moving well even on my bad side. I was riding better and feeling better after only a short time. I began to smile and then to giggle, tears of relief and gratitude sparkling in my eyes.

Peggy spent two days with Diva and me. What she did could be called "instruction" or "consulting" or "counseling." I call it nurturing. Peggy nurtured me as a rider and as a woman, and she showed me how to better nurture my horse and myself.

Diamond lifted her head and put it in my lap. It was a remarkable sight, the huge head settled on me and I

*rubbed her, stroked her, and wondered what her life had
been before this. Had people loved her as I was loving her
now? I brushed and curried her in spots that made her
lips stretch far out and her teeth made silent nibbles; I felt
then like we were becoming familiar with one another.*

Trish Maharam, *"Elegy for Diamond"*

IN MYTHOLOGY, THE horse is often associated with
fruitfulness. Odin's eight-legged mare Sleipnir embodied
fertility in Norse myth while a white horse takes form as a
Great Mother in the Buddhist Avalokitesvara of India and
the Kwan Yin of China. The naked lady on the white horse
whose legend was sanitized by the Puritans into the tale of
Lady Godiva and Peeping Tom was, in fact, a fixture in old
English planting festivals, where her ride in a public pro-
cession was considered critical to the fertility of the crops.
The Vikings looked to horses as well to ensure the earth's
fruitfulness. Their steeds were believed to be imperson-
ations of the clouds and the health of the crops a product
of their hoarfrost and dew.

In all these and other legends, horses are associated
with the nurturing act of conception. In real life, horses
give us an opportunity to engage in the nurturing that follows conception—the day-to-day caregiving that promotes
a healthy soul. Neither my current mare, Theo, nor I have
borne offspring, yet we both experience the need to nurture and be nurtured. When we are together, we are not so
different from any two women who are close. Each of us
senses the needs of the other and, like the best of friends
and mothers, reaches out to meet them. Trish Maharam
writes about this mutual nourishment in her essay on her
horse Diamond. "It dawned on me how different it was to

love an animal," she says. "There are no expectations in the giving."

IN THE RING or on the trail, Theo looks after me. There are times approaching a jump together when we come into the obstacle a little bit off our stride; she adjusts and makes me look good. There are other times completing a jump when I have not properly adjusted and we risk a fall; she saves me by making the adjustments herself. During our cross-country runs, the mare listens and watches and gauges the trajectory we need to sail over the fences safely. When she is lying in the field, I sometimes join her in the grass, resting my head on her side. I have known horses who were more outwardly affectionate, openly licking and nickering in ways Theo doesn't. But Theo and I try things out together, and, when we succeed, she embraces me by twining her head and neck around my body.

I support Theo in return. Rare is the day I visit her without an apple or carrot in hand. She stands peacefully as I greet her with a hug and a caress. In the barn I brush her body, comb out her mane and tail, wipe her face down with a soft towel, clean out her eyes and nostrils with a damp cloth, pick out the dirt and rocks from her feet, stretch her limbs, and massage her muscles. On warm days I often take her to the wash area, tune the water temperature just right, and give her a cool-water bath. She drops her head and her tail, bends her ankle, and sets one hind foot to rest, dreaming while the warm liquid bathes her in acceptance.

When we work in the round pen or on the lunge line, I encourage Theo's wild nature. I am pleased if she lets out a few bucks, throws her head and tail up, and struts around snorting and blowing. It tells me I have given her the space and time to replenish her wild energy. She needs that energy release through her body before she can fully enjoy our time as partners. When my horse and I are working together, she receives my space and my weight on her back with balance, trust, and calmness. In turn, I honor her needs by allowing her to fully express who she is.

She is merlot and ocean.
She is twilight and winter sky.
She is lilac and china.

She is crushed leaf and thin air.
She is mountain haze and blueberry.
She is amber and slate.

She is grackle and jay.
She is ink and lake.
She is steam and 'cicle.

Once orange.
Pink throughout.
Darkness fell in.
Cold came out.

Hard on the ground.
Forest and sand.
Lightness touched down.
Lava and fountain.

Joined in air.
The perfect being.
Lands with us.
Crimson here.

Sapphire cave.
Steel in stone.
Tailwinds blow.
Always in the eye.

A natural blend.
Spiral music.
Dappled plum.
Cardinal sky.

Mary D. Midkiff, *"Horses Are Purple"*

MANY HORSE OWNERS shy away from mares because they are more sensitive and temperamental than geldings. I'd be the first to admit that the hormonal quirks of my horses haven't made them easy, but I also take satisfaction from interacting with mares that I don't take from my relationships with the boys in the herd. Mares require more of a commitment because their physiological cycles make them less predictable and consistent. They need their human partners to be sensitive, compassionate, and patient if they are to fulfill their potential. Mares are also more complex than geldings, who have been altered to eliminate sexual drive and all its bad-boy ramifications. As a woman, I relate to a mare's complexity. I understand when she has big mood swings or down days caused by her cycle, or when she gets excited at seeing another mare with a foal. At times, being around Theo feels like looking into a mirror. I watch her struggle in ways that I struggle, and we overcome our difficulties together.

One of the first impressions Theo made on me was that she was protective. Even before I met her personally, I noticed her worrying over her pasture mates; whenever one of them left her sight, she would pace up and down on the fence line, calling and working herself into a lather until they returned. She still has her favorites among her herd at the stables, and she follows their movements attentively. When I ride her ahead of a line of other horses, she constantly looks back, making sure nobody falls behind.

Theo defines leadership as nurturance, a distinctly equine perspective. In human society, leadership and nurturance are often at odds. Although there has been some movement toward identifying and incorporating "feminine" skills such as consensual decision making into business, nurturance is not a term often used in the same breath with leadership. When it gets airtime at all, the impulse to mother is more likely to be the stuff of cartoonists and comedians.

Not so among horses. A herd leader who fails to nurture is no leader at all. The alpha horse is expected to lead the way to pasture and water, to alert the others to danger, to make sure nobody gets left behind. The stallion is a fine decoration and sexual partner, but the herd wants a mare at its lead. Horsewoman and author Susan Boucher says, "She may not be the biggest or the strongest, but she's the wisest, with a self-assurance that inspires confidence. If the lead mare is relaxed and grazing, the others eat, and if she startles and bolts, the others follow. In the landscape of horses, spookiness is in fact a virtue. The mares, among themselves, determine hierarchy—not only their own, but that of their offspring."

*B*ald Stockings was a good mother; the colt grew fast, and as the summer drifted by he learned the lessons of the range: how to stick close to his mother's side, so as not to be stepped on or knocked down when the band of mares was galloping; how to give Stowaway a wide berth; how to keep one eye always on the watch for prairie dog holes; and also about wolves—that was a terrifying experience. One hot noon, Pinto lay stretched out asleep on a hillside; Bald Stockings gradually had grazed on fifty yards down the swale. The foal never knew exactly what happened. There was a snarling rush which knocked him over as he scrambled to his feet. He heard his mother squeal, and the next thing he knew she was striking and biting at a gray thing that writhed on the grass, while another gray streak vanished over the ridge. It was over in a minute, and the mare, with nostrils flaring and a red light in her great wild eye, was nuzzling the still dazed foal. The gray thing on the grass was still; but before they trotted off to join the band the big mare shook it like a rag, while the foal huddled against her.

Charles Elliott Perkins, *The Pinto Horse*

AT THE END of each day at Theo's stable, the mares in her pasture line up in single file at the gate to be taken in for the night. They do not huddle and push for dominance the way children often do on a playground; but instead wait their turn in an orderly fashion. The number-one mare in Theo's group happens to be the oldest; she stands sentinel no more than a foot from the gate. Each mare occupies her own spatial territory and is careful not to trespass on any other mare's as she waits her turn to be taken in. The order never wavers or changes.

What I notice most about Theo moving within this system is her innate sense of where she belongs. She knows herself and feels comfortable with her place in the herd. If forced from her zone, she panics. Occasionally I go out as the horses are waiting to be led to the barn and bring her in myself, past the more dominant mares. She rushes past the grande dames to make sure she protects herself but also to show respect to the hierarchy of her pasture. It's as if by hurrying, she is saying *I swear I wouldn't be doing this on my own*. For that brief moment, I become her alpha mare and my presence reminds her that I am there to lead her safely past any mares who might be angry with her for disrupting their perfect queue. She resettles herself in the security of my company, and together we create a new temporary ring of comfort.

All of us have a place within our herds. Some of us are leaders; some are not. Many of us lead in one setting but not in another. What I have learned from Theo and the other mares at her barn and in other barns I have known is to find a place that is right for me in every herd I join and then to be comfortable there. I, too, have a circle of comfort. While it may not be as obvious as Theo's, it is just as real and it requires my respect if I am going to function at the highest levels within my own kind. My tendency early in my career and in my personal life was to be impulsive. I would bolt for the head of every line without much thought as to what I could contribute or whether it was the right place for me. I wanted to control and lead, but I found through trial and error that my contributions weren't always productive. With maturity and a life partner with a gift for patience, I have learned to watch and wait, as Theo does. Leadership need not make a lot of noise to be exercised.

Students as they are of nature, Native Americans long ago looked to the horse as a model of how to lead. To assure her son's mastery of horses, a Navajo or Apache mother would tie his umbilical cord to the tail or mane of a horse, where it remained until it wore away. "An Apache mother would bury the cord in a horse track, so that her son would be always industrious and devoted to taking care of horses," according to LaVerne Harrell Clark's Native American myth, *They Sang for Horses*. "Babies of either sex were often fed mare's milk to bring them good health, for the Navajo in particular believed that mare's milk was superior to cow's milk for building strong and sturdy muscles, bones, and teeth."

Time may have passed since those days, but the horse continues to teach us all about nurturing and leadership and how the two relate to one another.

*W*hen she awoke the next morning, there standing over her, sound asleep, ears flopped down and lower lip hanging shapeless like a bag of curd, was the old gray mare. Gretchen was as glad as the redbird singing over her head. She jumped up and, as soon as she had washed her face, ran to the mare and tried to get on her. But the old mare was too tall. Then Gretchen grasped her by the mane and tried to lead her to a log that lay near at hand. If she could get the old mare beside it, she could use it as a stepping block. But the stupid old mare would not budge. After vainly pulling, coaxing, and jumping about for a long time, Gretchen began to wail.

She was leaning against the shoulder of the old mare sobbing, when she heard swift hoofbeats, rhythmic and racking. She looked up and saw coming out of the bushes the beautiful White Steed. The sunshine was on his whiteness. He came arching his neck and pacing with all the fire of a mustang emperor, but there was something about him that prevented Gretchen from being in the least frightened. On the contrary, she stretched her arms towards him and gave a childish "oh" of welcome. He paced right up to where she stood, gently grasped the collar of her dress and the scruff of her neck in his teeth and lifted her upon the mare. Then he must have told the old gray mare to go home. At least she went. . . .

J. Frank Dobie, *"The White Steed of the Prairie"*

IN LONGMONT, A few miles from where I live, I have a little sister. We are not related by blood but rather by the connections arranged by the Big Brother, Big Sister organization. Coincidentally, my little sister's name is Mary. I see her every two weeks. We go to movies, make pottery, take hikes and picnics, and bake. She particularly likes to visit the barn with me and feed Theo a carrot or two. She puts on my helmet and gloves and walks around the barn, pretending she's a horsewoman while I groom my mare.

It is my intent to enrich Mary's life with the hours we spend together, to teach her the leadership of the horse. It is also my desire to enrich myself. Being nurtured is not enough for me, no matter how perfect my nurturers are. I need to nurture, as well. Nurturing reconnects me to my mother and to Peggy and to all my mares and the others who have bestowed the gift of nurturance on me. It leads me to a lush meadow where, like the instinctive mare, I graze in the warmth of the afternoon sun and feed myself in primal ways.

TRANSFORMATION THROUGH COMPASSION

As I soothe you I surprise wounds
of my own this long time unbothered.
As you stand, scathed and scabbed,
with your head up, I swab. As you
press, I lean into my own loving
touch, for which no wound
is too ugly.

Linda McCarriston,
"Healing the Mare"

*I*n the Celtic tale of the golden apples, Prince Conn-Eda must fulfill a seemingly impossible quest if he is to preserve his inheritance and become king. A friend gives Conn-Eda a magical horse to counsel him along the way, and, together, they overcome innumerable obstacles.

When at last they reach the gates of the city where Conn-Eda must secure the objects of his quest or lose all, the horse tells the prince to extract from its ear a small knife and "with this knife you shall kill and flay me." He tells the prince to envelop himself with the hide and enter the city but then immediately return to drive away the birds of prey feeding on the carcass. If "any little drop" of the powerful potion *ice* that the prince is carrying remains, he is to pour it on the horse's body. "When you do this in memory of me, if it be not too troublesome, dig a pit and cast my remains in it," the wise little horse concludes.

Conn-Eda protests that he cannot repay his horse's faithful service by killing it. "Come what may—come death itself in its most hideous forms and terrors—I never will sacrifice private friendship to personal interest." The horse is insistent, telling the prince they both will die and never meet again unless the young man follows his orders entirely. The prince at last reluctantly obeys, kills the horse, and falls into a stupor. When he revives, he sets out in desolation for the city. Only after he enters the walls does he remember the secondary promise to drive away the carrion birds and apply the magical *ice* to the remains of his friend. He rushes back to complete his vow.

The potent ice had scarcely touched the inanimate flesh, when, to the surprise of Conn-Eda, it commenced to undergo some strange change, and in a few minutes, to his unspeakable astonishment and inexpressible joy, it assumed the form of one of the handsomest and noblest young men imaginable, and in the twinkling of an eye the prince was locked in his embrace, smothering him with kisses, and drowning him with tears of joy. When one recovered from his ecstasy of joy, and the other from his surprise, the strange youth thus addressed the prince:— "Most noble and puissant prince, you are the best sight I ever saw with my eyes, and I the most fortunate being in existence for having met you! Behold in my person, changed to the natural shape, your little shaggy draoidheacht *steed! I am brother of the king of this city; and it was the wicked Druid, Fionn Badhna, who kept me so long in bondage; but he was forced to give me up when you came to consult him, as my* geis *was then broken; yet I could not recover my pristine shape and appearance unless you had acted as you have kindly done."*

Anonymous, from *"The Story of Conn-Eda"*
(or *"The Golden Apples"*)

FASCINATION WITH THE alchemy between horses and humans is as ancient as the two species. Conn-Eda with his stalwart "*draoidheacht* steed," Cinderlad with his seven foals, and Demeter changing herself from woman to mare in order to elude the pursuit of lusty Poseidon are all part of a long folkloric tradition in which humankind and horsedom meet and metamorphose. Often at the heart of these fables is a hero or heroine who has been trapped in a horse's form through enchantment and who escapes only when a kind soul at last recognizes the humanity beneath its coat and frees the captive spirit within. Almost inevitably, the liberator is enriched by this act of compassion. To transform is to be transformed, the moral of the story goes.

In my teenage years, I worked at a number of breeding farms around central Kentucky to learn more about horses. These were hard-labor jobs of mucking stalls, baling hay, sweeping barns, doctoring ailments, feeding and turning horses out to pasture, and cleaning endless yards of harness. Of all the horses I met in those years, it is the one who was most trapped that has never left me. She was a large, older Thoroughbred broodmare. Every time I entered her stall, she flew at me with her teeth bared, her tail swishing, her ears pinned, and her back feet flying. Despite her behavior, it was my job to feed and water her twice each day. The farm manager was an old hand of the sort who admonished, "Don't be afraid of her! Show her who's boss!" He'd enter the stall flailing a rope at the mare until she retreated, trembling, into a corner while he put her feed in and checked her water. The minute he turned his back to leave, she lunged at him; he always managed to escape just in time.

My instincts told me this mare was in crisis. Force and

violence were the language her handlers used with her, and force and violence were the vocabulary she learned to speak. I questioned whether there was an alternate approach to which she might be receptive—one of kindness and understanding and acceptance.

I was firmly told she was mean and best left alone.

I had a job to do, and the mare was only one of many horses I cared for. Eventually I was given permission to leave her feed and water outside her stall door, where someone more fluent in the harsh language of domination could carry them inside. In this way, I extricated myself from a volatile situation, but the experience did not end there for me. Long after our brief relationship, I continued to wonder whether it was possible that a princess breathed within the tortured form of the broodmare. I suspected that transformation had been possible, and I wished I'd known the way to set her free.

"*Drop* your stirrup so I can adjust the length. It's a little too short for you."

Kit didn't move.

"Kit, drop your stirrup."

"I can't."

That was true. Her leg was frozen solid with fright.
"Sure you can." Chloe stepped back and turned her head
away to light a cigarette. "Kit, if you want to learn to
ride, you have to trust me."

"It's not that I don't trust you."

"And trust the horse."

"In English, this substitute read us this poem about a
girl getting thrown and breaking her neck. Like they say,
shit happens."

Chloe took her time and blew a perfect smoke ring.
Shit indeed happened, unpredictable and everlasting.
"This gelding is twenty-seven years old, honey. The only
place he goes fast is to sleep."

Kit still didn't believe her. "Bullshit. What about that
senator that got crushed, or that guy who limps around
here feeding the goats?"

"If you're that sure disaster's right around the corner,
you have no business being up on the horse. Dismount."

"Well, maybe I could try it. Maybe."

"I'll just go over here and finish my cigarette. Let me
know when you've made up your mind."

Chloe went to the railing of the arena fence and
climbed up. She could see Kit's shoulders squared up
around her neck, the tremble in her double chin. Any
minute now, there would be a flood of tears and the lesson
would be over before it began. She tapped her cigarette

ash into the sand. Somewhere along the way, maybe one of her hip mother's interludes into communal living, thank you, this little girl had been badly scared by something, not necessarily horses. But getting on the back of a thousand-pound beast was one way to bring it to the surface. Whatever it was, she had to wait Kit out. She smoked her cigarette slowly, enjoying each breath.

Kit hung her head. Chloe climbed down from the fence, stepped back up to the saddle, and reached to stroke the gelding's neck. He nickered with pleasure. "Old Elmer," she said. "He's a fool for neck scratches."

"Chloe?"

"Bend over just a little and pet him."

"Are you sure you've got me?"

"Absolutely."

Kit moved her torso forward, and the leg in question slipped an inch. Chloe quickly slid the buckle down three holes and stuck Kit's toe back into the stirrup and stepped back. "Now ask him to walk."

Kit looked down the broad buckskin head with its scraggly, chewed brown mane. "Okay, you can walk now."

The gelding cocked a rear leg and dozed.

"See?" Kit wailed. "What did I tell you? This won't work. I'm fat, clumsy, ugly as a dog's butt. Forget the whole thing."

Chloe flipped her cigarette into the damp sand and heard it sizzle. Any more rain and this arena would be soup. Her mended boots could barely keep the dampness from her toes. "I can see you don't speak horse." She tapped the riding crop she was holding against her boot top, and Elmer perked up. A lesson horse from age twelve

*on, he knew the cues. He'd come to the stable nameless
and overweight, lazy enough to sleep through Chernobyl
unless someone stood in the ring holding a riding crop.
Three hundred bucks later, Chloe had saved him from the
dog food people. She never regretted it; she could put a
baby on his back, turn him loose in a field of cranky dia-
mondbacks, and he'd step quietly over them, one at a
time, deliver his rider to his chosen destination without so
much as an errant footfall.*

*She pressed Kit's heel into the gelding's barrel. "We
start with lesson one. This tells him he's got the green
light." Next she made a kissing noise. "That tells him to
step on the gas."*

*They moved forward. Elmer was wiser than he looked.
He knew who he could fake and who would call him on
it. But the two of them were moving forward, and Kit was
starting to get the smile back.*

*"Chloe! Look at me! I'm making him go! I'm rid-
ing!" Chloe stood back and watched them circle the
arena. If you were a doctor, sometimes you got to walk
into the waiting room and tell the people, yes, she's going
to make it, and if you were a teacher, maybe there were
times you saw the concepts sink into the gray matter, but
a riding instructor only had moments such as this one,
where desire to master overcame fear, and she savored it.*

Jo-Ann Mapson, *Hank & Chloe*

THE FANTASY OF magically metamorphosing into something new lies at the heart of fairy tales from Cinderella to Pygmalion to Disney's version of "The Little Mermaid." Horses bring the fairy tale to life. A woman on horseback grows in strength, speed, and mobility. She is Frau Gode leading the hunt on her white horse in German fable, the Norse goddess Mani driving her Alsvider across the night with the moon, Velvet streaking across the finish line to victory. On a horse, a woman is reborn as a mounted Valkyrie who until that magical moment lived only in dream. She is a savior riding to set spirits free, her own among them.

I have seen horses transform humans and humans transform horses. I have myself been moved and altered in these transactions. It is one of the reasons I ride and spend time around horses. For most of us, transformation is pretty much a matter of chance or luck. We discover the transforming power of an experience or person or event only after we've inadvertently stumbled through it. Horses give us a chance to *seek* transformation by giving us a partner so challenging and engrossing that it is difficult to be involved with the horse and not be touched in significant ways.

For those of us who seek personal growth, horses can be a catalyst that helps us stretch to become less fearful, more powerful, more in touch with our sensual selves. When I become involved with a horse or introduce another woman to horses, I can predict with some assurance "This will change me" or "This will change my friend." I cannot necessarily envision the change that will take place, but I can be sure it will come.

One of the most dramatic demonstrations of the horse's

power to transform is its effectiveness in physical and emotional therapy. The Lift Me Up organization in Virginia and the Colorado Therapeutic Riding Center near my home here are only two of the many nonprofit and private-practice groups putting the horse to work healing people. Groups like these provide facilities, horses, equipment, and staff who pair physically, emotionally, and mentally disabled patients with horses that can help them overcome their challenges. "The motion and warmth of the horse aids in normalizing muscle tone and stability, and improves coordination, reflex action and motor planning," the Riding Center explains in its literature. "The undulating movements from the gait of the horse are transferred to the rider and provide a rich source of stimulation. This stimulation enhances sensory input, improves the rider's respiration and circulation, enhances the rider's awareness of the position of his/her body in space and improves coordination."

And these are only the physical benefits. In their book, therapists Adele von Rust McCormick and Marlena Deborah McCormick write of dramatic turnarounds in the emotional lives of patients brought into regular contact with horses. One young boy who was determined to kill himself with a shard of glass stopped at the corral to say good-bye to his horse before carrying out his desperate act. When the youth climbed over the fence to talk to the horse about his troubles, opening his hand to reveal the glass, the horse butted the open hand with his head and knocked the glass to the ground. "David dissolved into tears and ended up staying with the horse, crying himself to sleep in the corral," the McCormicks report. "With the boy at his feet, Trianero stood watch like a sentinel. When dawn broke, it was not just a new day for David but the beginning of a new life."

He hasn't got any legs;
That is, he hasn't got

Any legs that work:
He was made that way.

He has to be dragged along
Like a rag doll. (Glad Rag Doll)

He is thin and pale
With storm-black eyes,

Living in a world
That does not speak.

Sometimes he screams.
Is it in protest?

Or is it some primordial force
Unknown to us that tears him?

Billy remains calm,
Lending him legs,
Sharing dumbness;
Raising him up

To look at trees and clouds

Until there's no more time for play.
His hands drop from the reins,

Embraced by waiting arms,
Rag Doll (Sad Rag Doll)

Is taken back to his chest
And riding is over for the day.

Robin Ivy, *"Child Rider"*

TINA BECKLEY IS one of the family therapists who volunteers to work with patients at the Colorado Therapeutic Riding Center. She has seen many new lives emerge as a result of horse therapy. Tina describes a nine-year-old boy who suffered from mental illness aggravated by the terminal disease of his mother. "I used the horse as a tool to help him refocus," she says. "When he got on the horse, he learned to enjoy himself in that moment and to think of nothing else." This temporary retreat into the soothing equine world helped the boy cope better with the harsh realities of his life.

When I visit the center, I can almost see the reshaping that takes place when an adult or child feeling crushed by her own burdens sits high on a horse's back. At least during those moments, peace seems to displace competing cares. One young rider told me, "It makes me feel good when I ride. I forget about being in a wheelchair. I have something really special that I can do that most people cannot." Horses have a gift for elevating their riders in more than physical ways and then returning them to the ground with a lighter load and greater confidence than they took into the saddle. When I see this, I see a soul beginning to move in new directions.

The horses chosen for the special work of places like the riding center are gentle souls themselves—good-natured pensioners or unusually patient companions. As they carry their riders toward healing, I like to think they do their jobs with compassionate hearts. There are many forces capable of transforming the human spirit, but few among them are as potent as compassion. "Compassion" is not an unthinking act of babying or indulging but a habit of paying enough attention to understand and relieve the suffering of another being. It is sensitivity, forgiveness, kindness, unselfishness, delicacy, tenderness, mercy. Compassion is an act that reveals itself by its effect. It makes no difference whether a horse or a human is on the receiving or giving end; compassion releases the finest attributes that lie within us all.

Like people, horses have individual ways of surviving in the absence of compassion. I have seen horses sink within themselves and other horses wear their emotions on their haunches. Some horses become conniving and manipulative in the absence of kindness; others, like the broodmare, violent; still others, dull and indifferent.

The absence of compassion is a brand that a horse wears as surely as a working animal bears its rancher's mark. People are no different. It is a rare person who doesn't bloom in the sunshine of kindness and understanding and wither in the darkness of indifference. As it does to the heroines and heroes of myth, the absence of compassion is a dark spell that can lock us away in an unrecognizable form until kindness sets us free.

She heated Drummer's wash water on a gas plate in the boss's office. She'd never think of washing him in cold water. She washed him with the warm water and the sweet scented soap and dried him carefully bit by bit with the towel. He never committed an indignity on her while she washed him. He snorted and whinnied happily throughout the washing. His skin rippled in voluptuous delight when Evy rubbed him dry. When she worked around his chest, he rested his tremendous head on her small shoulder. There was no doubt about it. The horse was madly in love with Evy.

Betty Smith, *A Tree Grows in Brooklyn*

I CAN'T RECALL the details of my first meeting with Iolanthe. At the time, I was a student at the Potomac Horse Center in Gaithersburg, Maryland. The mare's name would have appeared as one of many school horses on the list posted at evening chores during the beginning phase of my Horsemaster's training. Like dozens of students before and after me, I was assigned to ride her for a class session or two before moving on to the next horse on the assignment sheet.

It was a result of my own foolishness that I came to know the horse intimately. When I completed my studies in the assistant instructor course, I became eligible for the Horsemaster's certificate, the horseman's equivalent of a teaching credential. As part of the program, each student was issued a horse as a project. We all continued to ride a variety of horses, but the project horses were the ones we rode daily, groomed, bathed, and cleaned up after. They were "our" horses.

My project horse was a mare named Festival, a liver-chestnut with a pretty head and silken tail. At first we worked together in the indoor arenas because the weather outside was forbidding and the ground covered with snow over ice. When winter took a break and gave us a day that was warm and sunny, I couldn't resist taking the mare for a long, hard ride outside. It was exhilarating but careless of me, and we both paid for my excess of enthusiasm over common sense. Festival went lame from the hard pounding on the frozen ground. She had to be stall-rested for months while she healed. My credibility and status as a horsewoman in the program and in my own eyes sank.

It became my job to walk the lamed horse in hand while she healed as well as ride and train my new project horse,

Iolanthe. Not only did this arrangement double my work; it also left me with a dismal substitute for classy Festival. An Appaloosa, Iolanthe had worked for an extended time as a school horse before we met, a role that meant she was passed from thoughtless beginner to thoughtless beginner without ever feeling a consistent hand or being allowed to exhibit her own spirit. The experience had turned her sour, and her discontent showed from her nose to her tail. On her long face, she wore what seemed like a permanent sneer. Her ears were pinned back in a hostile expression of her general opinion of the world. Her coat was dull and coarse, her mane sparse, and her tail what horse people call a "rat tail." Her body sagged with discontentment and shame. Just as bad as her looks were her manners. When I rode her, she bucked and tried to run away. In company, she nipped at people and other horses. I was embarrassed for my new project and myself, but I was in no position to complain after pushing Festival to injury.

There may have been resentment in my heart, but I knew I could never let it show in my hands. Every day took me to the barn to groom, saddle, ride, and clean my penance horse as diligently and kindly as if she were a queen. In no time at all, my purgatory revealed itself as the horse's little piece of heaven. With consistent, gentle attention, a new mare began to emerge. Wrinkles in her nose relaxed. Then her eyes softened. Her ears began pointing forward instead of pinning back. Her posture lifted and lightened. She became quiet in the stall while I worked around her, and the nips and fussing stopped. Even her coat, originally so coarse and dull, began to shine as the once-mottled hairs blended into one slick, black spread of velvet.

It turned out the mare was an excellent jumper who was willing to try anything and everything. Iolanthe was metamorphosing from a disgruntled school horse into an athlete, and her metamorphosis was changing me at the same time. Soaring over jumps and flying together across the open, green fields of Potomac hunt country, it is hard to say which of our spirits rose higher. By halfway through our five months together, Iolanthe was gaining weight in all the right places, muscling up, and rounding out. She carried herself with an air of pride, she was happy to go on the bit and eager to go to work.

Meanwhile, I was riding better than I'd ever ridden before. At the end of our training, we were required to complete a challenging cross-country course together. We finished the course without a fault; I couldn't remember when I'd had so much fun on horseback. A friend who had been away from the program for some time witnessed our exhibition and asked me afterward, "Who are you riding?" She found my answer hard to believe. Like the Iolanthe who became a fairy in Gilbert and Sullivan's operetta, my horse had assumed a new and sublime form: Like Conn-Eda, I had been enriched as a result.

Moe Wilson, the manager of her own commercial trail riding business in the mountains of Colorado, recounts that she sees horses transform people every day. Moe is a passionate horsewoman at thirty-five. She says she knows the power of the horse in human relations because she experienced it herself as a teen. Whenever she felt like running away from home or misbehaving, she ran instead to her horse. They would talk. He seemed to understand and calm her down. She says, "Horses saved my life. Now it's my turn to show others how rewarding life can be."

She has opened her life and business to youth groups and organizations dedicated to underprivileged children from the Denver inner city. She says she marvels at the kids when they arrive at the stable, wide-eyed and full of curiosity. By the end of each ride, each horse seems to have brought out something from within each rider—an excitement that was trapped within or a new sense of calm. Moe enjoys watching the shy ones begin to interact and gain confidence; the more hyperactive individuals relax and receive the peace of the forest. But most of all she revels in seeing kids learn to communicate with another living being. A disaffected teenage girl might volunteer to work there; a fatherless boy might feel connected again. Moe sees herself in the youngsters, longing to have purpose and feel needed. Horses were the catalyst of the transformation. Young lives are infused with commitment, responsibility, communication, nurturance, and compassion through Moe and her horses.

My horses understand me tolerably well; I converse with them at least four hours every day. They are strangers to bridle or saddle; they live in great amity with me, and friendship to each other.

Jonathan Swift, *Gulliver's Travels*

HOW CAN A person tell if a horse is happy? There are physical signs. And emotional ones. A happy horse is an accepting horse.

When comfortable, the horse moves with fluidity, shows alertness without fear or tension, kicks up his heels, rolls in the mud with knickers of pleasure, and dances in place with his eagerness to work. He lowers his defenses and may even doze despite his inborn habit of being alert to possible threat.

There are less obvious communications, as well. A happy horse gives a hug by wrapping his neck around his human, gently nudging her with his head, neighing when he hears her familiar voice. He accepts the care of other people that his owner introduces him to because he wants her approval. He invites her into his life and asks her to stay.

Happy is the woman who hears such an invitation and answers *yes*.

Happier yet is the woman who learns that the same tenderness in her human relationships fosters cooperative and happy partnerships throughout her life. Our human companions and we ourselves relax and lighten with compassion's touch.

I felt better quite soon; the horse in gait and temper turned out perfection—all spring and spirit, elastic in his motion, walking fast and easily, and cantering with a light, graceful swing as soon as one pressed the reins on his neck, a blithe, joyous animal, to whom a day among the mountains seemed a pleasant frolic. So gentle he was, that when I got off and walked he followed me without being led, and without needing anyone to hold him he allowed me to mount on either side. In addition to the charm of his movements he has the catlike sure-footedness of a Hawaiian horse, and fords rapid and rough-bottomed rivers, and gallops among stones and stumps, and down steep hills, with equal security. I could have ridden him a hundred miles as easily as thirty. We have only been together two days, yet we are firm friends, and thoroughly understand each other. I should not require another companion on a long mountain tour. All his ways are those of an animal brought up without curb, whip, or spur, trained by the voice, and used only to kindness.

Isabella Bird, *A Lady's Life in the Rocky Mountains*

HER NAME WAS Marilyn. She was a slight woman, with dull hair that hung limp around her face, oversized glasses, teeth that were visible in their artifice, and large, heavy breasts that seemed a barrier between her and the world. She showed up at my display booth at a large annual equestrian show in Columbus, Ohio.

"I've had horses for seventeen years, and I'm still not riding," she confided when her turn came to consult with me about her issues with horses. "I'll go out and hop on one of them occasionally, but I always feel like I'm going to fall off, and sometimes I do. When they go slow, I have a hard time finding my balance to stay on." Marilyn was pained and embarrassed to confess she was living a few feet from horses and couldn't ride them. One aspect of her reaction especially confused her, she said. "I have a friend whose horse is crazy and loves to go fast, and when I get on her—even though the horse is wild and scary—I feel like I can stay on. And I do! How can that be? I don't understand."

Marilyn didn't understand, but many years had passed since my days with the furious mare and with Iolanthe, and my understanding of how women and horses relate to each other had expanded exponentially with their passage.

"What I think is that when you go fast, your body connects with the sensation of being part of one big movement, of blending together in motion," I told her. "It's like the feeling you get when you ride the round-up at the amusement park—the one where the floor falls out from under you—or when you stand in a subway train or fly in a jet. The vehicle starts out slow. You feel each movement in your body, and you adjust to each tiny little sway. It's a little uncomfortable. But as you pick up speed, the adjustments become slighter and slighter until you feel weightless and you don't have to work at all."

I suggested that Marilyn close her eyes and seek her center of balance—the position in which she felt the greatest sense of security—within her own body. This was an exercise Peggy Cummings had performed with me and that I had long since been sharing with other women. "You have to become familiar with your own body," I told her. "You have control over every element of your body, your soul, your mind, and your spirit. In the beginning, you and your horse were in tune with these elements. Maybe those natural abilities got buried along the way. Now you have to reconnect with those elements if you want to join yourself with your horse."

I stroked Marilyn's back and encouraged her to think of the long muscle that runs from the neck to the sacrum, to imagine it as relaxed and supple instead of tense and rigid. I took her fingers and laid them on the muscle so she could learn how her own body felt. I helped her align her spine in a position that felt more natural to her. Even as I spoke, she began to sink, her stiffness draining away, pliancy replacing the tension. At her side, twenty of my own years fell away, and I was in the barn again with Iolanthe, seeking to free a trapped spirit. "Have you found a secure place within?" I whispered. "Have you found the place you can hold, even if I come up and jostle you?"

She opened her eyes and nodded slowly.

Without further warning, I gave her a slight bump. She stood secure. I came at her from another direction. She didn't bobble. A smile stole across her face.

We worked together for quite a while as Marilyn practiced finding her center of balance and I persisted in challenging her. She went to her hotel that night and repeated the drills she had learned, then returned the next day—bringing her husband and friends to experience for themselves what she had. When she finally said good-bye, the pain and embarrassment so evident only a day before were gone.

"Seventeen years I've been waiting for this," she said.

I suspected there was a healing power in compassion from the days of my frightening stint with the furious mare, but I never tested my suspicion until I worked with Iolanthe. When I graduated from the Horsemaster's program, I was twenty-one and still a student of training horses. All the same, I had been the instrument of a transformation so complete as to seem magical. What I didn't fully understand then was that bringing about change in the mare would set off a transformation in me, as well. If I could find the winged victor in a sour, broken-down old mare, it occurred to me that surely I could release the higher spirit within myself. I didn't know at the time exactly what that spirit was, but I knew it was bound inseparably to horses and that I needed to do more than work at barns around Lexington if I was to realize its potential.

I returned to college after a two-year hiatus. The summer following my return, I traveled to Saratoga, New York, for the August racing season and caught my first glimpse of the horse world beyond Kentucky. I made new friends there and, like a parched sponge, soaked up yearling sales, morning workouts, afternoons at the track, and all the other horsy doings. Returning to the university that September, I interned with *The Blood-Horse* magazine and prepared yearlings for the next year's summer and fall sales at Keeneland and Fasig-Tipton. I even acted as a bloodstock agent on a few racehorse transactions and competed in college equitation programs, where I won awards as a rider.

I pursued possibilities I had avoided for years—finishing my education, breaking off a long and pointless romance, and seeking a future beyond the Kentucky state line. I didn't know yet where it was carrying me but my feminine spirit was rising. My own transformation from an awkward child on a fence rail to a woman of strength and assurance was under way.

I have been fortunate in my relations with horses and with people. I count among my fortunes the experience of putting compassion to work and bringing about change in others and in myself. Real life, of course, is not as simple as the fairy tales. In the end, no amount of compassion can free a spirit that prefers to remain captive, as some damaged spirits do. Nor is transformation a one-stop job. None of us, horse or woman, remains at our best if they are not well cared for. Just as I don't go through a day without checking on Theo's well-being, not a day passes when I don't look inside and check my inner balance to make sure I'm managing my life in a manner that brings out the best of me.

I have tried to make compassion a life habit. I think of it as practicing magic.

SPIRITUALITY

There was thunder in its nostrils and lightning in its legs; its eyes shone like stars and hair on its neck and tail trailed like clouds.

The rider spoke: "I know your people are in need. They will receive this: he is called Sacred Dog because he can do many things your dogs can do, and also more. He will carry you far and will run faster than the buffalo. He comes from the sky. He is as the wind: gentle but sometimes frightening. Look after him always."

Paul Goble, The Gift of the Sacred Dog

One scene in Virginia Woolf's *Orlando* always exerts a kind of magic on me. The setting is seventeenth-century London. The British aristocracy is hosting a winter carnival on the frozen Thames. Party guests arrive by horse-drawn sleighs hung with bells and swinging lanterns that part the thick fog and darkness for occupants who huddle under mounds of fur, only their rosy noses and cheeks showing. At the celebration, partygoers skate, dance, drink, and feast by torchlight until dawn approaches. Then the guests are carried away by the trusty steeds who have patiently awaited the command to go home.

Horses are always a part of carrying me home. Whenever I revisit this winter scene, I feel them take me to a place of warmth and safety once again.

No matter what kind of childhood we pass through, most of us remember parts of our early lives as being magical. It is one of the great endearments of youth that anything new may seem wondrous and even unimportant traditions can become treasured. Certainly if we celebrated

Christmas and the celebration included the Santa Claus tradition, Santa's bounty was magical. But many other experiences were, too. Every new discovery—about nature, about the world we lived in, about our bodies and our selves—held the potential of giving us that tingle of magic's presence. For some of us, rituals held magic. Specific sights or smells could evoke it, or even certain people. As children, magical possibilities were limitless. *Anything* could happen, or so it seemed.

Then we grew up and the magic faded. The world became more familiar and less surprising. The moments of wonderment and delight so common in youth become fewer and farther apart. For many of us, they stopped altogether. The fact that literature is full of tales about the poignancy of outgrowing magic is testimony to the universal sense of loss experienced when wonderment ebbs away.

Perhaps this is why, as adults, many of us seek passage back to the magical places of childhood. We practice rituals and traditions that once brought us wonderment or that elicit it from a child we know: We dress up and tell ghost stories at Halloween, string lights at the holidays, hide eggs at Easter, replace a child's lost tooth with a shiny new coin. When mythical characters dance across our television screens in commercials, we recognize that the advertisers are shrewdly trying to capitalize on the sway that the heroes and heroines who inhabited our youth still hold over our hearts and perhaps even our wallets. With a new generation of children, we reenact events and experiences that we ourselves cherished as children. One of the things I loved about having my husband's children around when they were young was the excuse they gave me to watch the wonderful early animated movies and read once more the tales that transported me when I was a child.

After all, what would have been the ultimate miracle for many a young girl? A pony under the Christmas tree! Okay, so it's not practical. Magic rarely is. All the same, in womanhood, horses do seem miraculous. They lift us up, fuse our bodies and motion into theirs, and take us places we could never go alone. Our legs become one with their legs and through their eyes we see a natural world we may have stopped seeing long ago.

> *Since childhood we have all had encounters with the Classic Horse. It is the horse of our dreams, fanciful and airborne, with a long flowing mane and tail. Its nostrils flare, displaying an inner spirit as magnificent as the mighty wind. It is the waves of the ocean and the fire of the setting sun. It saves us from the world. This mythic horse has marched forever through time with humans. This enduring image is a catalyst, opening us up to new horizons and teaching us about our inner feelings, the doorway to intuition. The Classic Horse rings in our psyche like a church bell; its overtones reverberate and linger, long after the bell has rung.*
>
> Adele von Rust McCormick and
> Marlena Deborah McCormick,
> *Horse Sense and the Human Heart*

EVERY TIME A horsewoman mounts a horse, she feels at least a tiny buzz of anticipation that's akin to the tingle of enchantment. Throughout her body, the cells of her muscles and joints and sinews sigh and smile and whisper *Ah, yes!*

We remember this! There are precious few things we do in adulthood that are near-exact reenactments of what we did in childhood. Yes, we eat family meals, but now we prepare them instead of simply sitting down to them. Yes, we enjoy family holidays, but now we make them happen instead of simply marveling as they effortlessly unfold. Yes, we see movies, but they are ironic and knowing and often grim instead of filled with hope and innocence and happy endings.

But riding—though it may mature and become more expert or more technical—remains a constant: The woman takes the reins, she mounts, she settles herself, she moves forward, she halts, she pats her partner, she dismounts. Instead of speaking with the tools and words of human communication, she speaks to the horse through her movements and her spirit. In the exchange, she regains her wonder, and her wonder replenishes her. A fellow horsewoman, Tina Beckley, tells me, "Horses are a break for the soul. I don't focus on anything else when I'm on a horse. I am in the moment all the time. When the horse calls to me way across the pasture, I am called into his world."

Horses of myth and legend often are associated with journeys. Some, like the *draoidheacht* pony in the tale of Conn-Eda, are magical partners on literal journeys. Others, such as the Celtic horse goddess Epona, are divinities who carry their humans on spiritual treks. It is a horse who carries the Navajo sun on its daily passage across the skies and a horse that pulls the Norse moon through the night. In Hindu religion, the planet's Apocalypse begins when the god Vishnu's white winged steed strikes the earth with its hoof, sending the entire world spinning on its ultimate spiritual journey of rebirth.

When a woman brings a horse into the journey of her

life, she takes a guide into a realm beyond her material existence. A horse knows nothing of his human's overdrawn checking account or the latest crisis in Washington or the fact that his rider's car made an alarming knocking sound all the way to the stable that very morning. The horse knows only that the sun broke through the clouds shortly after he was fed and that its rays warmed his stall. Released to his pasture, he feels his hoof strike the muck of damp earth and knows that water fell from the sky while he slept inside. When a flock of great honking birds passes overhead, he knows without knowing where his knowledge comes from that the cold days will soon pass and there will be more mornings like this one, when the sunlight caresses his withers and the earth offers him moist grass. He is neither grateful for nor discouraged by such discoveries. They are what the day has given him, and he lives them without thought. If the unexpected intrudes, he looks within himself to determine whether the intrusion is recognizable and whether he should stay with it or leave his comfortable spot and seek another. Whatever his decision, he does not look back.

A horse receives each new moment with accommodation or change. Regardless, he accepts new moments as part of the flow of life.

*W*e will not leave you yet. We will take you there. *The red pony threw her head, whinnied at the wind.* I will take you there.

First the song of the white horses, now the voice of the red pony. Goddesses all, in the old tales, yet tricksters, too. The goddess horse of legend would lure a rider onto her back, then transport the unsuspecting traveler away to the Other world. The rider might die to this world and all the people in it. The challenge could also be a simpler trial; a person brave enough to face death would be granted strength enough for life on this earth.

Brenna trembled. She must decide. In another heart- beat the moment would pass, Samuel's chance for life would be gone.

Squeezing the tears from her eyes, she let the rein looped over the pony's neck slip from her fingers. Rowan surged and wheeled eastward under her, the mare's pow- erful shoulder pressing against her left leg. Yielding fully, Brenna flowed into the horse, her breath and heartbeat one with the pony's.

Together they ran on, until they disappeared into the yawning mouth of the prairie.

C. A. Bauer, *The White Horses*

WHEN I RIDE Theo, this is the world she takes me to. My focus turns inward and my emotions turn on. When I am with my horse, I feel more than analyze, move more than ponder, accept instead of judge.

Her unity with the outside world is so absolute that I have no choice but to follow her into it. I must stop think- ing about deadlines and the grocery list and the clinic I'm scheduled to give next month, because they have no place in the world my equine guide is showing me. I can't help but open my eyes to what she sees and my ears to what she hears. I note the flicker of a cottontail disappearing into the brush ahead and hear the call of the meadowlark before spotting it. I swim in her quiet.

As minutes tick by to the rhythm of Theo's hooves, my

most timid inner voice begins to speak. It is timid because it is accustomed to being drowned by the clatter of the world I live in away from Theo. With a horse in my company and a horse in my consciousness, I am guided. Alone with this guide mare, the voice raises itself to remark on the beauty and variability of the creation around me, on the difference even a slight breeze feels brushing my bare arms, on the fact that spring smells like a greeting while fall holds the scent of things past. I find myself reassured that, no matter how much my material world changes, the world Theo takes me to offers constants I can return to again and again without ever wearing them out. Making my way through a moment with my horse, I am reminded of what is enduring and what is only passing, and this reminder helps me put my daily challenges into healthier perspective.

While we are journeying, Theo's animal spirit envelops me. Her breathing rises to match my breathing. Her animal warmth becomes my warmth. If Theo weren't carrying me into her moment, I could find a moment of my own, but it would not be the same. It is in part the softness of fur against my skin, the sparkle of her coat in the sun, and the warmth of her existence warming my existence that lifts me out of the corporeal world and gently sets me in a spiritual one. I become the goddess who is alive to the fullest only when astride her mare.

You leave the world that you're in and go into a depth or into a distance or up to a height. There you come to what's missing in your consciousness in the world you formerly inhabited.

Joseph Campbell, *The Power of Myth*

ONE OF THE spiritual riches that has been wrung out of modern life is the luxury of meditation, which takes the form of prayer for some people but takes many other forms, as well. Meditation offers us an oasis of rest from the spiritually parched stretches of our daily travels. It is an act that calls upon us to set aside the mundane and immediate and seek the mystical and universal. To me, the essence of meditation is any personal time given over to reflection that feeds the soul, a time—in the words of aviatrix and author Beryl Markham—when "I think, I ponder, I recall a hundred things—little things, foolish things that come to me without reason and fade again."

Horses give us a place where we may meditate. I recently participated in a workshop on creativity and empowerment for women in the second half of their lives. Each workshop began with a period when we were to turn inward in a way I was unaccustomed to: within walls and in human company. With practice, I was able to find my quiet place in this new setting but, whenever I succeeded, I felt as if I were with Theo! In Eastern cultures, people often create altars in their homes or visit shrines where they meditate. What I have learned about hallowed places is that my altars and shrines are where horses run.

Their road was through a pleasant country; and Fanny, whose rides had never been extensive, was soon beyond her knowledge, and was very happy in observing all that was new, and admiring all that was pretty. She was not often invited to join in the conversation of the others, nor did she desire it. Her own thoughts and reflections were habitually her best companions, and in observ-

*ing the appearance of the country, the bearings of the
roads, the difference of soil, the state of the harvest, the
cottages, the cattle, the children, she found entertainment
that could only have been heightened by having Edmund
to speak to of what she felt.*

Jane Austen, *Mansfield Park*

As A YOUNG girl, I passed many companionable hours
in the grooming ritual of brushing a girlfriend's long hair.
I recall twin girls in my elementary school with matching
heads of thick, long, wavy hair. During recess, I sometimes
brushed and plaited one mass of dark brown hair or the
other, while the twin of the moment daydreamed. In those
hours, time seemed to stop and nothing mattered as much
as the silken strands between my fingers and the faint
crackle of static electricity that erupted each time my brush
returned to my friend's crown for another trip down the
cascade of her hair. Hairbrushing was a ritual of young
friendship that soothed both the giver and the receiver. It
stopped sometime in my teens. Now I reenact it with Theo.
When I repeat over and over the simple motion of combing a finger through the mare's tail, I stop time as I did
then. In the comfort of the ritual, I smooth knots from my
own mind and heart.

Theo brings many such rituals to my life. Some riders
resent the chores that horsemanship requires, but others
think of them as a ceremony of friendship and respect.
Grooming is a central and intensely social act throughout
the animal world, a form of intimacy with meaning to both
parties. When I groom Theo, when I massage her, when we
talk quietly in her stall after a particularly good workout,

the motion and sameness of the routines become a holy act. Performing them, I renew my commitment to her and feed my sense of well-being.

Then we began to ride. My soul
Smooth'd itself out, a long-cramp's scroll
Freshening and fluttering in the wind.

Robert Browning, from *"The Last Ride Together"*

THE INDIAN SPIRITUAL and political leader Mohandas K. Gandhi said that fearlessness is the first requisite of spirituality. I like to think he was pointing out that until we face life and our own hearts with confidence, we will lack the courage to venture beyond the concrete and familiar into the more intangible realm of the sacred.

Theo and my other horses have not made me fearless. I'm not sure I know anybody who is totally without fear. But my horses have led me toward fearlessness. The physicality required to work successfully with a horse has given me confidence in my body. The uncanny way horses reveal my feelings and nature, good and bad, has conditioned me to candor with myself and others.

Horses put distance between me and the trepidations that might otherwise lay hold of me. In their company, I feel my apprehensions falling away and my spirit rising on the updraft of growing confidence. I look around and find I am no longer tethered to earth. The cares that weigh me down are temporarily lifted. I touch the clouds and hear the whispers of the divine.

In tribal cultures, there is a recurrent theme of humans coming into the world under the stewardship of a specific animal that confers its own characteristic strengths upon its host. No doubt I was born under the stewardship of the horse. The attributes I wish for myself are the attributes I find in horses: power, athleticism, confidence, respect, honesty, trust, sensitivity, calm, peace, and a capacity to be at rest and ease in an outdoor environment. When Theo is excited, she seems to grow with her excitement: She arches her neck, she prances. When I am dancing or animated by excitement, I think of the spirit and energy of my horse, and I will the same into my motions. By claiming her spirit for myself, it becomes part of me.

The horse is my talisman and my guide. It is the spirit I claim for myself and the leader I trust to carry me beyond my material world into a holier place. The horse is not every woman's talisman. For one woman it may be the cat, for another the bird, for still another a wild creature she may never see but can always dream of. We know we have found our own talisman when we touch an image or presence that lifts us out of our material world and carries us so high above it that we begin to see the threads that connect us to the rest of the universe.

How joyous his neigh!
Lo, the Turquoise Horse of Johano-ai [Sun],
How joyous his neigh,
There on precious hides outspread standeth he;
How joyous his neigh,
There on tips of fair fresh flowers feedeth he;
How joyous his neigh,
There of mingled waters holy drinketh he;
How joyous his neigh,
There he spurneth dust of glittering grains;
How joyous his neigh,
There in midst of sacred pollen hidden, all hidden he;
How joyous his neigh,
There his offspring many grow and thrive forevermore;
How joyous his neigh!

"Hlin Biyin" (Navajo "Song of the Horse")

from *The Indians' Book*

THEO IS A big horse. Each one of her twelve-foot strides makes about six of mine. My steps are short and choppy compared to hers, and, as a mode of transportation, they fail to move the world past my view as smoothly and panoramically. When I hike, as I often do in the glorious Rockies of Colorado, I have to look down and pay attention when I'm walking on my own feet. My own locomotion is a distraction. Riding Theo, I am able to enjoy every moment of my outing. She takes all the responsibility for picking the footfalls and keeping on the trail. She wears the hiking boots. True, I have to be there for her. I don't go to sleep (though, in truth, I probably safely could). She might spook at an unexpected movement or sound—perhaps a chirping prairie dog warning its buddies of our approach or oncoming llamas like the ones we once encountered that were on the trail wearing bright red backpacks. She may need me to reassure and calm her. But my being there for her only enhances our gorgeous solitude. When my mare and I are together on the trail, nothing and nobody else exists. Liberated, my spirit takes flight.

ACCEPTANCE

A horse appeared to me. It was a horse I had known from some long ago time. Who knows what that long ago was, but the horse was very present, and I could smell the horse, and the horse was very familiar. It seemed to be someone I knew from long ago, and so I felt I knew the horse well. I was very happy to see it, so happy that tears ran down my cheeks.

Interview with poet Joy Harjo,
Kalliope: A Journal of Women's Art

*T*ory was one of the mares I found for myself on the horse-gossip grapevine. She was a large, 16-hand, dark-brown mare of half-Irish descent. Her father was a Connemara pony stallion, her mother a good-looking Thoroughbred dam with an average racing record. Despite her good bloodlines, Tory was a mare with a reputation. Her former owner said she was not to be trusted. She was known to have dangerous stable vices. In the local horse community, it was rumored that she often reared and bolted while being ridden and struck out and kicked during grooming. Only bad stories popped up at the mention of her name—hardly a promising start for a new relationship. All the same, these are the circumstances under which we first met. A friend had proposed a trail ride for us from the farm where Tory lived. She had a horse of her own; the only horse available to me was Tory. A little dismayed but hungry as ever to ride, I accepted the arrangement.

My first impression when I reached the barn to saddle up the mare was how beautiful and feminine she appeared.

Although the warnings of other horse people were still in my mind, as the day unfolded I couldn't help thinking they must have been describing some other ill-tempered horse. Tory took me over the trails with ease and comfort and an attitude of genuine enjoyment. We galloped and even jumped a few logs without hesitation. We seemed to have started up a friendship, and my instincts told me that perhaps her behavior problems stemmed from the people around her rather than from her own nature.

I knew the family that owned her had little time to spend with her; as we returned to the stable, I began wondering whether I could make the horse my own. I finally had a well-paying job, and my future husband had recently offered to contribute to the purchase of a horse all my own. On the basis of that single ride and my intuition that Tory and I could accept each other and work together well, I approached her owners. They set a reasonable price and I arranged to buy her on a monthly payment plan.

Tory was my partner for the next five years, and our mutual acceptance made us a happy team. We rode in many hunts, horse shows, and horse trials. I witnessed the mare's rumored unpredictability only around cows, especially spotted ones; by imagining them as the misshapen mutations they must have seemed in her eyes, I came to understand the spooked reaction. Eventually Tory became the mother of my only foal, Bandit. Though Tory and I came to trust and love one another deeply, it was this brave colt who taught me the full range of acceptance—self-confidence, approval, faith, support, and, ultimately, accommodation to a sad reality.

Let us ride together,—
Blowing mane and hair,
Careless of the weather,
Miles ahead of care,
ring of hoof and snaffle,
Swing of waist and hip,
Trotting down the twisted road
With the world let slip.

Let us laugh together,—
Merry as of old,
To the creak of leather
And the morning cold.
Break into a canter;
Shout to bank and tree;
Rocking down the waking trail,
Steady hand and knee.

Take the life of cities!
Here's the life for me,
'Twere a thousand pities
Not to gallop free,
So we'll ride together,
Comrade, you and I,
Careless of the weather,
Letting care go by.

         Anonymous riding song
           "Songs of Horses"

BANDIT WAS A bay who was born with two perfect white rings around his eyes that made him look like a masked robber. The men at the farm where he was born weren't sure about the colt. They bred only Thoroughbred race-horses, and Bandit was a quarter Connemara. His mixed blood lowered his value in their eyes and made him an out-cast right from the start.

My foal's misfit status was reason enough for me to love him. I'd always felt confused about where I belonged. Kentucky bluegrass country is still a class-driven society in ways that few places in America are today. The success and reputation of my dad's hardboot father and the academic pedigree of my mother's family gave me the bloodlines to run with Kentucky's elite social horses, but my family had never reached the financial status required for us to join them. I could ride and train and compete as well as anyone but I couldn't afford a horse of my own; that simple dis-tinction ruled me off the grounds.

I grew up feeling as if I didn't quite belong anywhere—not in the middle-class horseless community or in the aristocratic horsy set—and every childhood and adolescent exclusion only reinforced that impression. My outsider status was perhaps best captured by my occasional role at the Lexington Junior League Horse Show. The horse show was and is a gilt-edged fixture in the Kentucky bluegrass community, a locally sponsored event of national magni-tude. My mom, a Junior League member despite our strained financial position, took me to the show every July afternoon and evening of its two-week run. I was a railbird and a dreamer and I sat in the trophy booth for hours on end, watching the hunter rounds by day and the Saddle-breds, Hackneys, and Walking Horses by night. On the weekend that climaxed with the crowning of the world's grand champion, I always wore my best dress, patent-leather shoes, and clean white gloves in hopes one of the official trophy presenters would fail to show. When that happened, I was allowed to fill the void.

One such summer night stands out in memory. The world's grand champion five-gaited horse was about to be crowned. As each competitor strutted around the large oval ring, the crowd indicated its choice with loud applause and whistles. The air was electric and the horses' sweat shone like the fur of slick young seals. In the trophy booth, I was fidgeting. The girl scheduled to present the trophy had not yet arrived. Struggling to hide my rising anticipation, I monitored the walkie-talkie buzz as show officials consulted about the trophy girl's whereabouts. I knew if she didn't materialize soon, I would be the one to carry the prize bowl into the spotlight.

When the announcer sang out the number of My-My, a multiple grand champion mare and everyone's favorite, the spectator stands erupted in approval. The mare, as she always did, responded by turning her glorious red body to the crowd and puffing herself up before trotting toward center ring where a ribbon would be pinned to her bridle and the sterling punch bowl presented to her owner. I think I grew an inch taller when the trophy chairman turned to me and said, "Mary Dike, would you like to take this out to My-My?" My eyes widened and I grinned as she handed me the bowl so big I could barely wrap my arms around it.

I was escorted to the center of the muddy ring by a man in a white dinner jacket, the star of my own Cinderella story come true. The faces of the crowd were lost to me in the lights. Time itself stopped. Every sound seemed muffled until My-My reached the greeting party. She could barely stand still long enough for the photographers to capture her; I could barely stand to keep my eyes and hands off her. Cameras flashed and then she set off on her victory trot.

The black-and-white newspaper clipping of my moment in the spotlight has yellowed a little at the edges but still nestles among my childhood treasures. When I look at it, I savor again its deliciousness but also taste bitter with the sweet. I was, after all, just the stand-in—good enough to hand out a prize if the "right" person failed to show but not qualified to compete or to be chosen as the presenter for my own merits. Childhood in bluegrass country was full of such reminders.

But how do you get the mare to accept a new foal? Paul remembered the man from Kentucky told him you had to familiarize the foal with the dam through a scent. "He told us he used to rub the colt all over with sheep dip. Then he'd rub the mare's nose with it, too. He'd trick her into thinking the colt was hers 'cause they smelled the same. . . ."

Marguerite Henry, *Sea Star, Orphan of Chincoteague*

BANDIT'S DUBIOUS CREDENTIALS didn't matter a bit to the foal's mother and me. We showered him with attention. Tory was a nurturing mom but, like most mothers, she was happy to have a good baby-sitter show up to give her the occasional break. While she napped, I brushed and stroked the young colt, lowering myself into the straw where he could nibble my hair and nuzzle my cheeks. Occasionally he'd try taking a nip of me, which only reminded me that he had a spunky and naughty side. Getting to know

Bandit was a new experience. I had groomed many year-lings for auctions by then and worked on many breeding farms, but this was different. He was my own child, and I wanted to influence his upbringing. Together we created our own intimate herd of two.

Bandit was a rambunctious young colt. As I led him from the barn to the pasture, he would often rear and buck. Once in the field, he tried to climb onto his mother's back and otherwise made quite a pest of himself. Tory tolerated such behavior for only a few minutes. Then she'd remind him of his place with a nip on his rump before she returned to her grass. One day the young horse was such a bother that his be-leaguered mom jumped a four-foot fence and joined the geldings in the next field in order to gain some relief. Tory was telling me it was time to wean our foal into adolescence.

The colt was five months old when I moved him to a nearby pleasure-horse farm where I could board him within my budget. A filly close to his age boarded there, and the two spent a few happy months together. They would graze side by side, frequently bolting into a run and kicking their heels when something startled them. Their favorite game was racing around the field trying to outrun each other. Bandit would probably have liked to stay with the young girl, but his hormones surged into action and he was shifted to an all-male field to keep him out of trouble.

The move wasn't easy for the youngster. First in his stall with his mother and me, then in their pasture with her alone, and finally with the young filly, Bandit had been part of a small and loving herd where he was corrected but rarely challenged and never rejected or abused. The big boys were not so accepting. In the world of horses as in the world of humans, there is always an acceptance ritual and a sorting of

any new member into position. It is often harsh and hurt-
ful. For Bandit, this meant watching the others form into a
pack that snarled and kicked if he tried to approach.

Observing from the fence rail, I could see my colt's
loneliness and confusion. I wondered if he would survive
the threats and warnings of the bigger horses.

> *In* every band of horses that have run together for any
> length of time, a line of precedence becomes established—
> a precedence as clearly marked among horses as it is
> among the diplomats of London or Paris. What the char-
> acteristics are that establish this precedence is not always
> clear—age, experience, strength, fighting ability, cun-
> ning, perhaps a balanced average of all. But anyone who
> will observe a strange horse turned in with a crew of
> horses that have run together for some time, will notice
> that in a comparatively few days the stranger will have
> found his level, often with no open fighting. There is some
> way in which horses can take each other's measure with-
> out actual conflict; and once that measure is established,
> unless man or some unusual incident upsets it, you will
> find that in the case of horses running undisturbed it is
> seldom broken.
>
> Charles Elliott Perkins, *The Pinto Horse*

HUMANS AND HORSES are both herd animals. In the
wild, a lone horse is almost assuredly a doomed horse—easy
prey for predators and the last animal given access to water
or forage. Even in domestication, an isolated horse often
will sink into deep depression and give up on life, ceasing
the movement that is vital to its well-being and literally
starving itself. Humans may survive better when separated

from the herd, but few of us thrive without the companionship of others.

Acceptance matters to all of us. It matters because we feel happiest and most comfortable when we are wanted and included and are sharing both our pleasures and our setbacks with others. It matters because rejection, as Bandit learned, is painful and frightening. It matters because the value others place on us has a way of coloring the value we place on ourselves. And it matters because, ultimately, we have to accept ourselves to reach contentment. Our horses do it innately; we have to work at it.

There are two things for which animals are to be envied: they know nothing of future evils or of what people say about them.

Voltaire, French philosopher and writer

HORSES AREN'T SO quick to give up on themselves. Faced with rejection, Bandit distanced himself from the other boys without totally withdrawing from them. He studied the natures of individual horses and learned which ones he could approach without risking a sharp kick or a stinging nip. He began to establish who he was as a horse among horses. He might have been immature and unpolished, but he seemed certain that he belonged and he was determined to take his place. He chomped grass alone for a few days but slowly edged nearer to the other horses. He didn't run away from rejection. Instead, deliberately and without show, he began working his way into the herd.

At his stage in life and long after it, I lacked the self-confidence to handle rejection from my herd members so bravely. Whenever I was left out of human crowds, I fled, seeking solace among horses. Horses know nothing of money, status, beauty, or accomplishment. They don't care who holds the papers to them as long as it's someone with a soothing voice, a warm hand, and maybe a carrot or two. Horses know who is gentle and who is harsh, who listens to them and who only commands, who extends compassion and who is indifferent. Horses see only our hearts, and they accept or reject us based on what they find within. In short, horses do naturally what humans can pass a lifetime without ever mastering.

Even so, one of the truths I have learned about myself since and suspected even then is that horses aren't enough. Over the years, I've held jobs that many a horsewoman would give a sound limb for, but the fact is that a lot of them were solitary jobs—six, eight, ten hours a day alone with horses. I love horses. I often think of myself as a horse. All the same, as often as I've turned to my magnificent friends for pleasure, comfort, and wisdom, I've learned I need a human herd, too. The search for a peer group—or two or three of them—is an experience that brings out still more colors in the coat of acceptance we all hope to find.

The boy stopped a moment, standing quietly. Then he squatted on his heels and went to work on the foal's face. "Look at me, Sea Star," he said. "When Misty comes back home, you and she can be a team. Misty and Star. Sound pretty to you? And you can run like birds together and you can raise up foals of your own, and Maureen and I can race you both and we won't care which wins."

*All during the ride to Wimbrow's, Paul quieted Sea
Star with his voice. Inside Wilbur Wimbrow's gate Paul
set the colt down on the grass. To Paul's surprise, he followed along to the barn as if an invisible lead rope held
them together.*

*Looking at the weak little colt, Mr. Wimbrow shook his
head. "Sure is slab-sided," he said. "Let's do something!"
He turned to Grandpa, "Ought we blindfold the mare?"*

*"T'ain't no use. Sea Star's about the color o' her own
colt. We'll coax in with him and put him right into her.
Maureen and Paul, you kin look on—if you back up
against the wall and stay put."*

*The stall came alive with expectancy. Mr. Wimbrow
tuned his voice down low. He was trying to make it sound
natural, but Paul and Maureen felt a tightness in it. "I'll
hold the mare's head so she can't turn round and bite," he
said. "Clarence, you put the little fellow where he belongs."*

*Now the mare filled in the silence. With a sound no
bigger than a whisper she began snuffing and blowing
and snuffing in again. She tried to turn her head.
Grandpa's head nodded yes. Mr. Wimbrow let go the rope.
The mare could turn her head now. She brought it
around slowly toward Sea Star, looking. Now her breathing was quick, as if she had just come in winded from a
gallop. And then in the middle of a breath came a quiver
of sound. It was like a plucked violin string. It was pain
and joy and hunger and thirst all mixed into one trembling note. She and the colt were one! A high neigh of ecstasy escaped her. Fiercely she began licking Sea Star's
coat, scolding him tenderly with her tongue all the while.*

Marguerite Henry, *Sea Star, Orphan of Chincoteague*

ONE SUMMER IN my early twenties, I was asked to consider preparing two prized yearlings for a husband-and-wife team of physicians who owned a historic farm in the heart of bluegrass country. The interview took place in their Scott County manor house, a vision with soaring ceilings, full-length windows, and a grand staircase. The three of us rocked in chairs on their large screened porch, gazing onto their endless acreage where shiny horses grazed inside perfect white rail fences as we talked. Iced tea was served, and we sipped it with fragrant mint sprigs as we spoke of the two yearlings: their pedigrees, dispositions, and experience with people and about what their owners hoped to realize for their sale.

As business was typically transacted among hardboots, no paper was exchanged. I was qualified and our families knew one another. That was enough. We agreed on pay and hours, took another glass of tea, and shook hands on our deal. I was given two months to teach the yearlings manners and bring them to peak condition for the highest price possible.

I should have been elated, and for a time I was. The yearlings were exceptional, and my employers were gracious and delightful people who welcomed me not only into their barns but into their home. I was not merely an employee; I was part of their herd. At last I belonged. But as I worked with the young horses over the following weeks, I made an unsettling discovery. I was fulfilling my dream of working full-time with fine horses, I was spending every day on a beautiful Thoroughbred farm, I was associating with lovely people in a gorgeous and historic setting. In short, I was no longer standing outside with my nose pressed against the candy-store glass; I was finally inside

the emporium. Yet I felt restless. The sense of completeness I'd always thought that taking my place in Kentucky's
horse set would bring me wasn't there. My dream had a
flaw. I just wasn't sure what it was.

I returned to college a summer after my brief stint with
the yearlings. As a young woman with a Horsemaster's certificate and considerable experience, I had been embraced
by many of Kentucky's horsemen by then, but the restlessness I uncovered on the Thoroughbred farm hadn't gone
away.

Acceptance was turning out to be a horse with a dappled
coat: Viewed from one angle, it showed one color; studied
from another, it revealed another. For most of my awkward
childhood and aching adolescence, acceptance appeared to
be a prize exclusively within the power of others to award or
withhold. When people around me no longer withheld the
prize, I saw it in another light. Acceptance, it began to appear, wasn't just a matter of winning someone else's stamp
of approval. It seemed I couldn't take my place in the herd
until, like Bandit, I was confident of my own worth.

Finishing the education I had abandoned after my
sophomore year was a step toward raising my value in my
own eyes, and my belated success as a student did just that.
When I was hired a few months later for a highly visible and
glamorous job gathering marketing data for a new horse-
training center in Maryland, I felt sure I had assembled all
the elements necessary for the sense of belonging and
completeness that had eluded me in the past.

The marketing position sent me traveling thousands of
miles to a dozen different racetracks, where I spoke with
hundreds of trainers collecting information to advance the
project. Everything about the work thrilled me: the travel,

the people, the horse-training philosophies and facilities I was exposed to. I collected a healthy paycheck for work at which I excelled and that carried me into a higher tier of the horse world. *This is it*, I exulted. I was doing what I wanted, where I wanted to do it, and I was doing it young. What a success story I thought I was.

Then it was gone. Just as the job was beginning to feel like the perfect home, funding for the training project fell through. Overnight, the position and all its perquisites vanished. One day I was a sharp young marketing executive making good money in a nice office where I could indulge soaring dreams; the next I was unemployed. I was devastated. Instead of seeing the event for the temporary setback it was and moving on, I lowered my head and skulked away, letting the loss of my job—the rejection, in my mind—undermine my self-confidence and self-value once again.

I fled to the herd where acceptance was always mine: horses. I took work as a show horse groom at a fancy Pennsylvania hunter barn where I groomed and exercised horses, cleaned stalls, and swept barn aisles. It was menial work compared to my glamour job, but it was comforting. I talked my options over with the horses—giving up on an equestrian career was high on my list—and shared with them my feelings of shame and loneliness. Their tireless patience soothed me and their unflagging contentedness in the face of my turmoil finally made me see that my troubles weren't so big after all.

In the stalls and in the fields, the marketing job and its effect on me took on still another cast. I had again been setting my own stock on the strength of appearances and the endorsement of others. I had essentially said *Now I have the perfect job; I don't have to work on me*. The trouble was that I'd invested my whole self-worth in my job; once it was gone, my stock was in deep trouble.

In the company of accepting horses, I felt humbled but hopeful. As they always had, the animals welcomed me into their herd irrespective of anything but the spirit I conveyed with my hands and my voice. They reminded me that my true value rested not in a job title or a surname but in my heart. Feeling complete, quelling the restlessness, finding acceptance was a prize I could award to myself, just as I had bestowed it on the grand horses at the Lexington horse show. It would gleam within me even if nobody else ever saw it. I just had to accept that I deserved it.

The weeks among the horses fostered that confidence. When a friend referred me to a better-paying temporary job opportunity at Princeton University after a few weeks, I was revived enough to sign on. For a change, horses weren't part of the job description; just this once, I didn't mind at all.

Shortly after Bandit joined the herd of big boys, I arrived at the farm one day to find that his handlers had returned him to the enclosure with the filly. More startling, I noticed he appeared to be drunk. He wobbled when he moved and seemed to have trouble standing.

When the vet arrived, he could find no injuries or cuts to account for Bandit's unsteadiness. We surmised that perhaps he had taken a bad fall in the deep mud of the field and sustained internal injuries. We made him comfortable until we could get a neurological specialist to examine him the next day. It was not until his examination was complete that I had an explanation for the sudden shakiness in my spunky colt. He was diagnosed with Wobbler's syndrome, a mysterious equine spinal disorder.

For several months after his diagnosis, Bandit was given

every chance to return to full health. Every few weeks the vet came to check his progress. He was given acupuncture treatments as often as I could afford them, and I gave him massages and stretching exercises. These made him more comfortable but they couldn't reverse the deterioration of his spine.

At seven months old, Bandit was developing into a beautiful horse. The rings around his eyes had vanished and his entire brown coat had been shed for a silvery light gray. I was sure he was to be my shining white event horse. However, it soon became evident the colt was not growing or improving. I learned of a horse angel, Margaret Watters, who was known for taking on problem horses. Bandit moved again, this time to Margaret's training center seventy miles from my home. The horsewoman walked him twice a day, gave him special seaweed supplements to encourage some growth, and stayed with him while he ate his feed to make sure he finished it all. I made the three-hour trip to visit him once a week and talked daily with Margaret and the vet.

My hope for him and for us was fading, and the colt's pain was showing in his spirit. He was bred to run and jump and perform. Instead, every movement hurt him. He began to hide with his head facing the far corner of his stall and, when I came to see him, he seemed unhappy with the attention. Bandit needed acceptance as much as he had when working his way into the herd, but he was ashamed of the shape he was in and of his inability to control his body. He didn't want pity or help; he wanted to shine and dance. When he couldn't, he shrank from contact.

My summer at Princeton was spent as the only female on a gardening crew of eighty-two men. I drove dump trucks, shoveled dirt and gravel, pulled weeds, trimmed roses, and mowed grass every sweltering day of the long mid-Atlantic summer. I was accustomed to hard physical labor from my work around horses, but it was an unfamiliar sensation to perform it shoulder to shoulder with hardy union men who would be quick to spot it if I didn't pull my share of the load.

Mowing and hoeing my way through the long summer gave me plenty of time to think about my lifelong quest to belong. Alongside my burly male coworkers, I uncovered inside myself a conviction that physical toil was honorable and satisfying—a piece of bedrock I'd lost in the glitz of my office job. I also found that the sense of independence I gained from supporting myself with hard labor mattered far more than the appearance I made. I realized I'd spent a lot of my life depending on the limited cachet of my bloodlines to open a few doors and feeling resentful when they didn't open all the right ones. I began to see the marketing job as merely another pedigree I'd relied on to set my value instead of looking to the qualities underneath. Sweating in the New Jersey haze, I felt a new sense of myself taking root, one that had nothing to do with pedigree, report cards, or job titles.

Animals hold us to what is present, to who we are at the time. What is obvious to an animal is not the embellishment that fattens our emotional resumes but what's bedrock and current in us: aggression, fear, insecurity, happiness or equanimity. Because they have the ability to read our involuntary tics and scents, we're transparent to them and thus exposed—we are finally ourselves.

Gretel Ehrlich, "Friends, Foes, and Working Animals"

from *Intimate Nature* . . .

IN MARGUERITE HENRY'S *Sea Star, Orphan of Chincoteague*, the foal's rescuers induce a mare to adopt the orphan by crushing leaves from familiar myrtle leaves and smearing them over the youngster's coat so it would smell acceptable to its surrogate mother. At Princeton, I could say I won acceptance from my fellow gardeners with the honesty of my sweat. My diligence on the job won their respect, and by the end of our summer together, they had accepted me as one of their own. I valued the high regard of these men, but something far more important had taken place in the university's gardens. At long last and not a moment too soon, I'd won the high regard of the most critical audience of all: myself.

I was twenty-five when I went back to college, a few years older than everyone else in my classes. For the first time in my life, I was the one consistently raising a hand to answer questions posed by the professor. After all, there was more at stake for me than simply a few credits; I was trying to earn my own respect.

Bursting with a newfound appetite for learning and personal growth, I decided the heady world of academia might hold a herd just right for me. I scheduled after-class meetings with my professors to continue our discussions and began spending more and more time at the library researching the engaging topics that emerged. I joined a women's literary group and took classes in women's studies. Like a mare settling into a new barn, I nosed through the herds of students and teachers looking for people who made me feel at home.

It was in a class on women's literature that I found a group I thought could be my own. The class was taught by a professor who both startled and delighted me. She was a diminutive, soft woman with skin that appeared never to have been touched by sunshine. Her hair was cropped bluntly just below her ears and finished off with little-boy bangs straight across her forehead. She had the voice of a mouse yet she roared with passion about her subject: female poets and writers. In fact, literature was the only force that seemed capable of bringing color to her cheeks.

I had never met or seen anyone like her before. She wore only shapeless, tentlike dresses and abstained from wearing jewelry and other ornamentation. The evidence of money that was so critical to acceptance in Lexington was absolutely missing in her manner and style. Yet she was respected and widely liked by the large circle of students who congregated, myself among them, in her class. Together we explored the feelings underlying the powerful and beautiful sonnets and novels of artists who, more often than not, were trapped inside the walls of society and their own homes. Our own stories spilled out, real and imagined woes were shared, and bonds began to form. For a time I was drawn powerfully to these women who were so much more engaged than the sleepy undergraduates that dominated my other classes. I threw myself into the course and was never without something to add to our spirited discussions.

In only a few weeks, though, I found my perennial sense of otherness surfacing again. I was different from my fellow students in fundamental ways—from the opposite physicality of our lifestyles to their opinions on people and life in general, I could feel a discomfort growing within me. I began to notice that my professor often seemed angry and almost never laughed. Increasingly, the passion for literature I thought we all shared began to reveal itself as more of a zeal for words and concepts that gave voice to their own considerable discontent.

I was accepted by the professor and other students but they were of a different breed. We could run together for a time, but I wasn't one of them any more than I'd been a member of the Lexington elite as a child. Even if they approved of me, I couldn't take a place among them and likely wouldn't have been offered one once my personal disposition was better known.

It was not enough merely to find inclusion within a herd; I needed to find a herd that felt like a home, not merely a watering spot.

Margaret Watters called and said she would pay for the surgery that was Bandit's only hope for wellness. She had fallen in love with my colt and felt compelled to try this one last option for saving him. We discussed the idea at length, and I agreed to her offer despite my embarrassment about accepting her financial generosity. During the surgery, it was discovered that Bandit had five lesions on his spine. One is sufficient to handicap a horse. He developed double pneumonia after the surgery, deepening his stress.

Bandit didn't deserve more stress. I gave the order to end his life.

My colt's life was exceptionally short for a horse, measured in months instead of years. In leaving so prematurely, Bandit taught me another aspect of acceptance: the ability to make peace not only within ourselves and among our fellows but also with our circumstances, especially those that cannot be changed.

Today I find acceptance within many types of people. I have found homes among horsemen and writers and gardeners and others. Sometimes I find what feels like a whole herd within the body of a single person. These are like the horses at the barn that Theo singles out to be her pasture mates. It took a good long while, but I finally claimed for myself what Bandit knew all along: that we have to believe in our worth, that we can work our way into a herd, that there's no sense in beating ourselves up when we fail, and that the ultimate acceptance for any of us is found beneath our own skins. Only then can we truly belong.

HEAVENLY HENRY AND MISSY

Several times in my life certain horses have entered to show me the way. Such was the case of an eight-year-old leopard Appaloosa named Special Venture. I did not own a horse as my husband's heart disease of long duration precluded extra expenditure. However, I was told about an App that nobody was riding and might be a fun project.

My husband and I went to look at him, and even though he hadn't had shots or been wormed for several years, he was a beautiful, kind, knowing, and elegant animal. My husband said, "I think you should get him," so I worked out an arrangement with the owner, subject to a good vet check, negative Coggins, and a five-day deworming before moving him. Each night my husband and I drove miles to visit the horse, worm him, and give him a bran mash just to keep things moving along. When the vet came and I rode the horse, he trotted out in small circles beautifully, so we didn't X ray him. My husband leaned against the car and watched. I have pictures of him from this time. The blood tests were fine, save the low white count from infestation, and we remedied that so I moved "Henry," as we both called him, to a friend's lovely farm. My husband's notes in his diary recount that day. Then I began trail riding him and my husband's notes say, "Missy rode Henry and he was great."

Two days later my husband suffered an abdominal aortic aneurysm and was raced to the hospital. For the next forty-three days in intensive care, as his life was waning, I rode Henry alone across the fields, crying and wailing my heartbreak and fears.

When my husband died, I rode Henry. Through the memorials and aftermath, I rode Henry daily, alone or with loving pals. Then one day, as I was slowly adjusting, Henry stumbled in a plowed field. He went down on his knees and then gained his feet again, took two or three very lame steps, and went on. "Something is very wrong with Henry," I said to my pals. "Nonsense," they all said. "He is fine." Still, I felt uneasy and called for a major X ray of his two front feet. Dr. Pryor took many many views of both feet and called the next morning. "Do not ride him," he said. "There are multiple fractures in the bones of both front feet. I don't know how he has done what he has for you."

But I knew, and I whispered my love and thanks to him that night. He knew, too, and the next morning he was put down and released to gallop the heavenly fields. No one else would subject him to hurt. And maybe he is the beloved mount for my husband in heaven. It would not surprise me, not at all.

Missy Warfield Hollingsworth
Versailles, Kentucky

SEASONS

I too live hot before the final flash
cavort for others' gain

We toss our shining heads
in an ever increasing standard of sweat

The mind deranged, Democritus
Who knows us, friend—
our indicator needles shot off scale—
Spinoza, Burns, Xenophanes knew us

in days when thought arose and kindly stayed—
All creatures whatsoever desire this glow

Lorine Niedecker, "Horse, Hello"
from T & G Collected Poems (1936–1966)

At Hartland, I spent part of every day possible in the weanling barn, visiting the babies. Between the time the foals were weaned from their dams to when they were sold at the Thoroughbred auction, they were known only by their lineage and perhaps a nickname. Unless the breeder decided to keep the foal and name him or her themselves, the foal's naming was a pleasure reserved for its new owner. There was one brown filly I particularly loved. I secretly named her Weeong. Every morning I walked into the barn and called *WEEEE-OOONG*, and she whinnied in reply. She would come up to the bars of the stall so I could kiss her fuzzy muzzle and pet her nose. Her soft breath was sweet and her eyes held nothing but love and trust. I was sure she was my little sister. I would feed her hay and talk to her for what seemed like hours. She grew into a beautiful yearling. We spent the summer together; I visited her every day, right up until the morning she was taken away to the September sales and a new home. I felt helpless watching her being trailered away, and, for weeks, I visited her stall to breathe in her scents and remember our talks.

It was always that way with the horses at Hartland. The seasons were set not by the calendar but by what was going on in the barn: breeding, foaling, weaning, sales. The mares were there to produce racehorses and generate revenues, and their babies were born, sold, and shipped like any commodity. I tracked the year by the swelling bellies and the departure of horse trailers sighing under a full load.

For most of my life, I have thought of myself as a horse and Weeong as just one in a long string of horse siblings. As a young girl, I was a foal; in my teens, an awkward yearling. During the years when I began to explore a wider world, meeting new challenges, I saw myself as a sleek and athletic racehorse, setting records on the track. Always as I reached each new season, I took comfort and instruction from other horses, the ones whose response to change was so much more instinctive than my own.

Today I am a mature horse, beyond my reproductive years. This season came earlier for me than for most women, in my late thirties. Unlike the warm earlier seasons, its arrival was surprising and harsh, like an unexpected cold front in the midst of Indian summer. I lost sight of my fellow horses and struggled to adapt. As so often has been the case, it was a horse who ultimately helped me find shelter and showed me the road again after the storm had passed.

Diva was the gift of my horse angel Margaret Watters. The ten-year-old mare came to me in a period when I was longing to compete at higher levels, and she seemed the perfect partner for my dreams. Her first owner had registered her with The Jockey Club for racing purposes as Feminine Woman; I didn't think the label suited either of us. I renamed her Diva, and a diva she was. On our first outing in dressage, she won her class. We finished first and third in two subsequent horse trials. We were on our way to becoming a successful partnership.

Our first spring together, Diva became preoccupied—as many mares do—with breeding. After consulting with her vet, I put her on medroxyprogesterone, a human contraceptive, and we soldiered on: showing, performing, and consistently placing in the ribbons. Diva performed beautifully on the hormone therapy, and the vets who supervised her assured me we could safely maintain her on it. I gave little thought to the interruption I was causing in a natural process.

By our second spring together, the hormone therapy was no longer producing a settled mare. When I worked with her in-hand on the ground, she stopped and challenged me as a stallion might in a dual. I couldn't even take her on a nice long trail ride without her trying to get rid of me. Her overall attitude toward work was one of reluctant acquiescence bordering on anger. It was as if she'd come up to a wall she couldn't see over, much less jump.

Diva broadcast her final signal that she was opting out of our partnership at a horse trials competition one early spring when her hormones were at high tide. After a tense and uncharacteristically poor performance in our dressage test, we began warming up over jumps for the cross-country phase of the trials. She was jumping nicely but there was an edginess to her that was not settling down within our exercises. Finally our number was called and we walked a few hundred yards to the starting box. In front of us, the wide, just-mowed grass of the green course stretched toward the distant hills, ready for our attack. We entered the starting box and turned in the direction of the first jump. The starter began his countdown backward from ten. When he gave us the final 3-2-1 to start, I nudged the mare lightly with my legs, usually all it took to send her flying. Instead, Diva froze. She raised her head, pointed her ears toward the course, but assumed the pose of a statue. I kicked her sides and urged her forward with my body weight without provoking a reaction of any kind. At last I smacked her flank with my crop. Still no reaction. I yelled, kicked, and gave her another swift whack. No result. My normally fleet mount had been replaced by a stationary fixture. As a last resort, I relaxed my efforts and tried talking to her. I coaxed her to walk quietly out of the box, make a small circle, and reenter. Inside I positioned her again to lunge toward the first hurdle, but she froze again. One more time I repeated the cycle; she remained unwilling to move forward.

I tipped my hat with my riding crop, the signal to the officials that we were calling it a day. We were eliminated. Friends hanging around the start area questioned what had happened. I patted Diva's neck, shrugged my shoulders, and walked toward the warm-up area without knowing how to explain.

Away from the competition course, we approached a small jump. Diva faced it eagerly and cleared the poles with little effort. I knew then that she could handle a jump on her own terms but not the high-pressure work that required her complete focus over a long period of time. Perhaps as she looked over the course, she heard an inner voice telling her she might get hurt if she wasn't completely present. Maybe she was protecting us both from injury. She dictated the outcome that day, not I. She was like an honest woman in the grip of overwhelming events: She re-

alized she couldn't get the job done that day so she pro-
tected us. Another day, maybe, but not that day. She was
smart enough not to push.

It was easy for me to sympathize with the mare. I had hit
a wall, too. Though I was only thirty-seven, the body that
served me so well for so long was betraying me in significant ways. Irregular periods, depression, anxiety, sore and
swollen breasts, fatigue beyond words, and lack of libido
had taken over. I felt as if I were undergoing the worst case
of PMS in my life—every single day.

My athletic ability suffered, and my emotions and
thinking were in turmoil. My riding, my marriage, my career, and my future were under siege. All the insights I had
gained about power and commitment and compassion and
danger, all the expertise I had gained in the horse world,
all of this and more were being drowned in the storm of
physical ill-being. The need to feel well again became
overwhelming.

I attacked the problem by taking myself to the woman's
version of the vet, the beginning of a long and frustrating
crusade. First the gynecologist and later a urologist and a
general practitioner pronounced me 100 percent healthy.
I was puzzled. How could I feel this awful and be perfectly
healthy? At one point my gynecologist suggested I was
imagining my symptoms. I felt insulted. I was certain a
concrete medical explanation existed for my discomfort;
instead of finding one, my doctor was suggesting my symptoms were in my head. The physicians' dismissive attitude
increased my feeling that I'd lost control of my life. I was
doing my best to take responsibility for my health and well-
being by seeking appropriate medical care, but the "experts" were brushing my concerns and efforts aside as if

they were pesky horseflies. The experience made me feel as if I were once again sitting on a fence rail, only now it was my own life I was watching pass by.

My frustrating experience with human medicine made me reevaluate Diva's experience with its equine equivalent. The mare's monthly cycles had interfered with her performance and training schedule. Putting her on medroxyprogesterone had evened out the hormonal fluctuations and enabled us to train and compete successfully, at least for a time. Now, however, she was behaving worse than she had before I put her on the hormones. I began to question the wisdom of continuing the therapy.

Eventually the vet and I agreed to take Diva off hormones. She improved but she continued to be ill at ease within her body, just as I was within mine. A number of seasoned racehorse trainers later counseled me on the use of hormone therapy in competition mares. It appears that hormonal regulation can be helpful in the short term, but usurping the natural chemistry and rhythms of a horse's life to accomplish human goals and objectives is counterproductive over extended periods. Diva had been left on the drugs too long; now we were both paying a price for my misinformation and resulting mismanagement.

It was during the search for an antidote to return Diva to her old self that I was directed to a therapist who practiced equine massage. Gwen Edsall was instrumental in educating me about herbal alternatives, like raspberry leaves, which are believed to help mares regain hormonal balance, and introduced me to massage, acupuncture, and chiropracty for horses. Almost every therapy she recommended for Diva had a corresponding therapy for me. I began experimenting with non-Western approaches to this season of life. While Diva took her herbs and homeopathic supplements, I drank my prescribed Chinese herbal tea made from sea urchins, seaweed, mushrooms, Chinese vegetables, and roots. Diva underwent monthly chiropractic adjustments and acupuncture treatments, but I allowed myself weekly sessions in my search for balance. We both improved, but my improvements were more dramatic. My body felt stronger and my energy level was restored. My faith in myself no longer seemed misplaced.

My outlook on my physical symptoms began to change, too. I took a look at the year on the calendar and finally acknowledged that a new chapter of my life story had begun. I was aging, and aging was bringing about change. I might still feel fresh and frisky but my cells knew youth was behind me. As a mature woman, I needed a new outlook—one of wisdom and discovery rather than intensity and invincibility.

About this time, Peggy Cummings—the woman with the unique language of horsemanship—invited me to participate in a riding clinic she offered in Idaho. The trip was my introduction to the vastness and grandeur of the West, and it was exactly the whole-woman treatment I craved. Under skies without ceiling and views without limit, I spent four days riding, exercising, and learning about my body and its evolving needs. Holistic healthcare experts presented alternative approaches to wellness. Between classes we worked with horses on the ground and in the saddle. I rode whatever was available: Arabians, mustangs, and Thoroughbreds, alternating between Western, Australian, and English styles of tack. None of the trappings mattered; I was there only to learn what mares know by instinct: how to survive and thrive when the weather changes.

*As I handled Steppin' that night, I tried to remember
the last time I dreamed about playing. I could remember
being a child and turning bicycles into charging steeds. I
made sticks into magic wands and sprinkled angel dust
from the moist earth. How powerful I was! How easy it
was to run to my friends' house and ask them to play.
How readily they agreed. How beautiful each leaf looked
as we stared, enthralled with the magic of it. I've noticed
that humans tend to outgrow these things. "I'm too old,"
we excuse. Steppin' is 20 years old now and I've been told
that's about 60 years as one of us. He doesn't know he's
"too old." No one has told him to stop doing these things.
Could we, even in middle age, learn to roll in the mud,
muss our hair and become feral too?*

C. J. McKague from *The Horse's Mouth*

I RETURNED TO Virginia feeling healthier and more
hopeful than I had been in memory. Over the ensuing
months, I followed the new regimens for self-care diligently and was rewarded with fewer symptoms and a growing sense of wellness. Eventually, even though I was still in
my thirties, I was diagnosed by a homeopath as being in
perimenopause, the transitional season between full reproductive life and menopause. By trial and error, I eventually developed a combination of conventional and
alternative medicines to pass healthily through this season.
As I did, the sense of helplessness the hormonal battles had
spawned began to subside.

Throughout this period, I continued to give Diva every
form of support I could find or imagine. At times she
seemed to be willing to participate, but we never returned

to the partnership we'd known a year earlier. At last I was forced to concede that Diva and I were on opposing calendars. This was Diva's reproductive time of life. She wanted a baby, not a career. My reproductive season was past; I was eager to explore a wider world. I sent the horse to Florida to a fancy breeding farm where she could enjoy her season with other mares like herself. The last I heard, she was happily grazing and awaiting the birth of a foal.

Left to her own nature, Diva would have moved smoothly and contentedly from competing to breeding. She would have accepted the change in signals her body was giving her and embraced them without the misery that was induced by the hormone treatments. Diva would no more have tried to override what her nature was telling her than she would have attempted to override winter with spring.

Looking back on my own change of season, I wish I'd picked up my own signals a little sooner and embraced the change of seasons with Diva's equanimity. I knew from experience that ignoring my body's signals—living and doing without consciousness—led to needless injury and distress, yet apparently I hadn't taken the lesson to heart. With a little bit more introspection and self-motivation, I might have investigated the signals and better prepared myself for the changes to come. After all, aging isn't nearly as much fun as those youthful seasons when we are finding mates or giving birth or setting new personal bests on a regular basis. As we age, self-awareness takes on a new relevance.

——for Mom

HOW OFTEN lately I've looked in a mirror
and seen you with my eyes—
not twin face and features,
but heart: a look alike copy
of what you feel for life.

Once, as a girl, you found a run-away
race horse near Maywood Park,
bliss-filled you galloped up and down
the cinder streets until
the authorities came
and took your dream away.

Always a finder of motherless things
you raised orphaned rabbits
and gophers,
swam the leech-ridden Des Plaines
hopped freights that took you west
to pick tomatoes all day for a quarter.

During my childhood I never
saw a wild rabbit
swam a river or
ate vine ripe tomatoes.
I saw the world from suburbs and Air Force
bases; begged you every Christmas for a horse.

Years grew between us.
I cultivated my own world apart.

Then, this summer, in the Bear Paw Mountains
I grew tomatoes for the first time
and rode all day in the wind
helping the hands sort cattle.

Feeling firm red fruit,
sun and shadow,
smooth rocking chair lope of the horse
I knew I'd found you,
in the heart
that binds us,
found in myself a re-creation
of your childhood dreams.

Laurie Wagner Buyer, *"Growing Tomatoes"*

238 \ MARY D. MIDKIFF

WHEN I FEEL myself fighting the climate changes, I remember a horse I once knew named George.

George was going on thirty the last time I saw him, making him about eighty in human terms. He was on the smallish side compared to many horses, a mixed breed of Morgan and Quarter Horse, chestnut with white stockings and a white blaze on his face. He wore a tremendously thick coat of fur that no longer shed out as it had when he was young; his owner always body-clipped him a few times each year to make sure George felt comfortable and his internal thermostat was in balance. The old horse no longer needed to wear horseshoes because he only traveled in the fields or indoor arenas, which were soft and cushioning to his slow-growing hooves. He couldn't trot for a long period without getting winded, but, when his owner rode him, he still seemed happy and proud to be working with other horses the way he once had. He made it clear that he enjoyed the attention of being groomed and saddled a few times each week, and he never tired of the carrots and apples offered to him.

When I asked his owner about George, she always replied that she'd had him checked by the vet and he was doing just fine. He was simply growing older but he was doing it with grace, as we would all benefit from doing. Good care made George's life easier, but the slower lifestyle and new tranquility of standing under a shade tree or lying in the sun came naturally to him. He reminded me of an old man who had lived life well and now was resting from his efforts, hands clasped behind his head, body rocking in a chair on a broad and cool porch where he could remember the past and relax in the present. George finally had time to enjoy what gave him pleasure. He loved to stand at the trough with his neck extended downward and his muzzle pulling water into his mouth. Sucking it in as he did, he was able to slosh the water between his lips for a few moments before sending it coursing through his body. He could close his eyes and feel the cool flow over his gums. He was in no hurry to guard his place in the herd or fight to get to the gate first. Let the young ones worry about all that. He might wander over to lean his behind up against a fence board and give himself a tail massage instead.

I lost track of George when I left Virginia, but, in my mind, he will eventually settle into a nap and drift off to play in green pastures where life is totally carefree. Many people have seen a foal born but few have witnessed a horse die of natural causes. The scene is a metaphor for life itself as gravity pulls this immense animal back to where it started. Seeing an animal die comfortably, in full acceptance of what has been and what is happening to it, can open our souls to a new way of looking at both life and death.

Old horses like George pass away with a grace and dignity that belies the trials of their lives.

I am definitely not ready to settle for a good scratch against a fence or drift off to carefree pastures, but I learned from George and other aging horses that there are pleasures to be found in a slower pace and a higher appreciation of what is immediately at hand. The change of season is inevitable, but every season holds its own delights.

My horse with a mane made of short rainbows.
My horse with ears of round corn.
My horse with eyes made of big stars.
My horse with a head made of mixed waters.
My horse with teeth made of white shell.
The long rainbow is in his mouth for a bridle
And with it I guide him.
When my horse neighs,
Different coloured horses follow.
When my horse neighs
Different coloured sheep follow.
I am wealthy because of him.
Before me peaceful
Behind me peaceful
Under me peaceful
Over me peaceful—
Peaceful voice when he neighs.
I am everlasting and peaceful
I stand for my horse.

Traditional Navajo song
From *The Navajo Indians*

IT WAS NOT long after Diva left for the breeding farm that Theo entered my life. Unlike my previous mare but like me, Theo's breeding days were past. We were both in our middle years and still are. These days we both use hormonal support to smooth the ups and downs. We both benefit from acupuncture and massage and stretching. I notice that, just as I do, she gets out of shape faster than she used to when we're not working hard, and she takes longer to get back into competition trim. As usual, Theo sets a good example for me. She's not as likely to push herself when her body asks for a rest, but she's not about to retire, either. My mare revels in her maturity and encourages me to do the same.

I used to ride because it fulfilled my need for speed and daring and strength. I love horses now as much as I did then, but in a different way. I no longer feel as if riding is a means to reaching a goal. Today I enjoy my horse and other horses in their own space and time. The older I get, the more I want to move through life's stages as they do. I thrill as they carry me past unforgiving human notions of getting old into a rhythm of life as certain and natural as time itself.

As I contemplate the seasons ahead of me, I continue looking to my horse angels for guidance. Margaret Watters was the angel who tried to help me save Bandit and who gave me Diva. She was already in her late seventies when I met her, but she was still exercising young racehorses as if her body had not registered the passage of years. Margaret had spent a lifetime with horses, both on the track and at home on her farm, and her dedication to their welfare was the driving passion of her existence. She did stop riding not long after we met, bowing reluctantly to the pressure of doctors and family members who argued that a woman so tiny and frail did not belong on horseback. She made the concession to age without heartfelt conviction. Horses were her life, and life must have seemed a strange and bland thing without the daily communion of riding them.

Knowing her heart as I did, it came as no surprise to me when I learned the circumstances of her death, a few years later, in her early eighties. She had a young friend who wanted someone to ride out with her when she tested a horse she was considering purchasing. Margaret volunteered to take a look. With the girl on the sale horse and Margaret on a stablemate, the two riders wandered out on the trails around the large country estate. Coming upon a low-lying log, Margaret instinctively did what she'd always done: She asked the horse to jump. The horse jumped the obstacle, but as it landed, Margaret lost her balance and fell to the ground. She hit her head and died instantly.

Like all those who loved Margaret and were warmed by her passion for horses, I mourned her passing. All the same, I couldn't help thinking that her life ended just as she would have scripted it for herself—with the wind in her face, the reins in her hand, and a horse under her rump.

JOYCE NESMITH AND A HORSE
FOR ALL SEASONS

My recent passage through menopause occurred during a particularly stressful time at work. I also took up
riding about the same time. I had no idea what was in
store for me and yet now I can say that the challenge of
learning to ride and becoming a horsewoman during this
period helped me immensely.

   When I'm on horseback, I have to live in the present. I
am with my horse. If my mind wanders when I am riding
and if I am not paying full attention to my environment
and my horse, I could end up in very unhappy circumstances. When we are together, I concentrate completely
on him. These moments in the present bring relief from
stress in my life. I have a great time trail riding. I love to
listen to the birds, look at the trees and plants, and watch
for deer, foxes, and other wildlife. I feel the rhythm of
Presto's gaits, feel his back and belly swell if he gets
frightened, feel it dissipate as he calms. All these sensations need to be acknowledged and synthesized while I'm
looking at scenery or deciding what direction to take
next.

   Learning to ride has been the greatest physical, mental, and emotional challenge I've faced in my life. Nothing in my school or work life can compare. Learning to
ride has required concentration, hard work, and persis-
tence on my part. I am convinced that having to muster
and focus all my forces on something positive outside

myself during menopause helped me through it. Riding Presto also presents frustrations at times. These moments in turn help me focus my energies on constructive ways to overcome frustration.

When my mother became quite ill about three years ago, my horse helped me during that time, too, by giving me an outlet where I can completely escape for a few hours. When I return to "real life" after riding, I am refreshed and ready to face the challenges. Being with Presto gives me peace. . . .

Personal account of Joyce Nesmith (1996)
Alexandria, Virginia

FREEDOM

$\mathcal{B}$ut the Phantom was not running a race. She was enjoying herself. She was a piece of thistledown borne by the wind, moving through space in wild abandon. She was coming up, not to pass Firefly and Black Comet, but for the joy of flying. Her legs went like music. She was sweeping past Firefly now. She was less than a length behind Black Comet. The people climbed up on the fence rails in a frenzy of excitement. "Come on, Black Comet!" screamed the crowds from Pocomoke. "Gee-up, Phantom!" cried the island folk. Maureen was no longer an onlooker. She was the Phantom winging around the curve, her nostrils fire-red in the dying sun. She was Paul, leaning forward in a kind of wild glory. She was drawing close to Black Comet. Now she was even. She was sailing ahead. She was over the finish line. She was a winner by a length!

Marguerite Henry, Misty of Chincoteague

A mile above sea level, the Colorado sky is an azure canvas. Walking Theo along the trail near her stable, a bald eagle soars over us, its head and neck a blinding white against the blue. A red-tailed hawk circles on an up-draft, etching a spiral into the heavens; a flock of migrating geese carves an avian arrow toward a destination far south. If we stay out until the blue darkens into black, I know the night sky may reveal even more—a young barn owl, perhaps, or a great horned owl.

Every winter raptors and other wingborne creatures come to Colorado to warm themselves and feast on prairie dogs and other animals easily spotted on the autumn-scraped landscape. The birds are an endless source of fascination to those of us who live where America's grandest mountains meet its greatest plains. Rising and diving and floating on invisible currents, the birds skim the countryside with grace and speed and an assurance any of us would wish for ourselves. From ancient times, birds have been a metaphor for freedom. They were wildlife sirens who tempted humans to seek a means of leaving earth. Men have died searching for the secret to flight.

Women know a better way to claim the bird's freedom. Women ride.

He was what every horse wanted to be. Can you imagine a horse with hooves of silver, a mane soft and thick as a waving cloud, a neck strong as a Roman arch and "clothed in thunder," a broad back smooth as lakewater, and an eye of pure fire? Well, if you've imagined all this—and it's more than most people could do—you would still have no idea of how Pegasus looked.

For in addition to all these perfections there was a greater one. From the shoulder-blades of Pegasus there sprouted two of the widest, whitest, most powerful wings that ever fanned the skies.

They shone like soft lightning, even in the dark, and great legends and splendid poems were written by those lucky enough to find one of the quill-feathers. Only the archangel Michael wore a grander pair, and even his, though rainbow-colored, were no swifter than those of Pegasus. Have you ever seen a hummingbird above a flower, balancing on nothing but air, its wings going so fast that all you can see is the tiny body darting like a living emerald? Magnify that a thousand times, change the quick green to alabaster-white and you'll have Pegasus—except that Pegasus was so much faster than a hummingbird as a hummingbird is faster than a tortoise. You can believe that such a creature would not stand to anyone's hitching post. Only the gods could put a halter on him; only the heroes and poets could ride him—and even they could not always keep their seats. Although he came down to earth at rare times, his favorite pasture was the sky, and it was no uncommon thing for Pegasus to bound from a river-valley to the highest mountain peak and then, with a sudden beat of those mighty wings, to scale the walls of heaven.

Louis Untermeyer, *"The Horse of Sienna"*

A COUPLE YEARS after meeting Theo, I decided to find out if she and I were ready to compete in a more rigorous sport than dressage. I went so far as to invest in a custom saddle made to fit her back and my pelvis, in hopes of furthering our chances of competing successfully. Theo was sixteen years old by then; I was forty-three. I didn't know if either or both of us could hold up to the rigors of combined training, which is also known as eventing. Competition would require us to take multiple jumps, very fast, over an extended period of time. It is a sport mostly performed by young athletes who have greater strength and heal faster from the demands on the body; by comparison, Theo and I were "seasoned" athletes, to summarize the situation gently.

I had not tested my still-developing relationship with Theo under the conditions of a cross-country training session that combines open country, varied obstacles, and speed. I couldn't be sure she would stay in focus with me, or whether she might mentally and physically run away. After all, she had raced for a couple of years in her youth. Our first training session would test more than our athletic ability; it could foreshadow any limitations to the scope of our relationship.

The first time we challenged ourselves, we trailered a short distance south with several other horses and owners to practice at an equestrian facility with an endurance course and jumps. Theo was well behaved while I tacked her up soon after our arrival. As we warmed up, she remained calm and well within herself. The course was a few fields from where we'd unloaded. When we reached it, Theo could see the jumps stretching out before us. She froze and stared into the distance, as if the sight had stirred old and dim memories of her competitive career years ago. Nonetheless, she remained quiet and cooperative. We took our turn going from jump to jump, one at a time, making sure we jumped in stride and safely. During the moments we waited for others to go, I reminded her with my voice and my body of our work at home, reassuring her that this situation was no different. We might have company, but, on the course, it was still just the two of us.

After clearing our fourth obstacle, several members of our group commented on how well behaved Theo was and what a professional she was being after such a long hiatus from eventing. These were all fellow horsewomen who knew our story and had watched the union develop after Theo and I reached Colorado. In their eyes, Theo was a horse who was at last coming under control. I knew she was a mare who had finally become free to fully express her magnificence and share it, uninhibited, with me.

The horses cantered over springy earth. There was a glory in riding. The human became part of the animal, attached by invisible wires; muscle connected to muscle and bone merged with bone. Epona felt the strength of the stallion become her strength; its speed and grace were hers, too. She sat on the powerfully thrusting haunches with her head thrown back and her eyes closed, not thinking just feeling, light and free.

Free. This is what it is to be a horseman.

Morgan Llewelyn, *The Horse Goddess*

ONLY TWO YEARS before that session, I had felt my safety at risk riding on the open road near the farm where the formerly explosive mare lived. Now we were enjoying ourselves far from home, in wide-open fields, and Theo was making me proud. My dreams of competing in eventing and of riding a desirable horse were at last taking substance. I said a silent thank-you to Helen Junkin, Theo's former owner, and knew she would beam when she heard of our success. The last group of jumps were in a long line, with no turns or dips to impede our speed. We covered the ground as fast as we could and flew over each obstacle. In her freedom, Theo gave me freedom, too.

After two more training sessions, I believed we were ready. I signed up for a competition sponsored by the United States Combined Training Association in Castle Rock, south of Denver. The event was set for a Saturday in May, beginning at eight o'clock in the morning. Shortly after daybreak, we were on the road.

I had always dreamed of walking to the starting box of a cross-country course on a fine horse, dressed for the occasion in riding helmet with green and white satin cover, safety vest and rugby shirt, my penny—a biblike vest—with my number and the name of the competition on it, prepared and partnered to take wing. In practice, Theo and I kept our speed and intensity in reserve. In competition, we would let ourselves go. Traveling south on the interstate, I felt excited but not nervous. After all, I had nothing to lose. No matter how we scored, the joy of performing with my horse was prize enough. I was at last going to do what I had always wanted. I was Epona, the Celtic horse goddess.

Freedom, Epona thought hungrily. Passionately. *Freedom such as the horsemen must know, sitting on those beautiful animals as they run across the . . . what was it called? The Sea of Grass? Imagine a sea of grass. Not sailing ships but galloping horses, and a horizon unlimited by mountain peaks.*

Morgan Llewelyn, *The Horse Goddess*

As Theo and I found our way down the hill toward the start box that day, I said to myself, *I'll always remember this moment*. And I do. I remember the sense of total readiness I felt and the pride of looking good as a team. The rolling hills were green from winter's snowfall and the skies low from an impending thunderstorm. These, too, I still see. The breeze was brisk but I don't remember any cold. I knew we'd be hot once the competition started, and we were.

Because of the threatening thunderstorm, the time between starts had been shortened from the normal five minutes to two. There wasn't long to wait once we reached the box before the starter sounded *Go!* and we made a clean, strong start.

Champing the bit, and tossing the white foam,
And struggling to get free, that he might dart,
Swift as an arrow from the shivering bow—
The rein is loosed. "Now, Bucephalus!"
Away—away! He flies; away—away!
The multitude stood hushed in breathless awe,
And gazed into the distance.

Park Benjamin, from *Alexander Taming Bucephalus*

The first jump was a simple wooden coop about three feet high. I'm an aggressive rider and I didn't hold much back even though I was anxious to set a smooth, steady rhythm from the first jump. We cleared it with ease. The second jump was similar in style, and we finished it as cleanly. At the third jump, I felt Theo slow and knew she was taking a long look at the obstacle. It was no higher than the previous ones but it was more solid—a stone wall with evergreen trimmings laid on top. On the other side, we would have to make a sharp left turn immediately. I felt the hiccup in my mare's confidence slow her gait. I cried out my encouragement and urged her on. When her hooves came down cleanly on the other side and we finished our turn, I felt her momentum surge anew. It never flagged again.

Who shall declare the joy of the running!
Who shall tell of the pleasures of flight!
Springing and spurning the tufts of wild heather,
Sweeping, wide-winged, through the blue dome of light.
Everything mortal has moments immortal,
swift and God-gifted, immeasurably bright.

Amy Lowell, "A Winter Ride"
from A Dome of Many-Coloured Glasses

THE FOURTH JUMP was the scariest—down in an overgrown swale and built out of scores of thin, light-colored bamboolike poles. We couldn't see what lay on the other side of it. But Theo trusted me to take her through and we sailed over, made the required turn, charged uphill, climbed an embankment, and cleared a massive fallen tree. We slowed, taking a rocky decline but once it was behind us, I turned her loose—inciting her to move as fast as her legs and heart would carry her, across the landscape and over the remaining hurdles.

We flew! We danced! We reveled as only best friends can. As we cleared the last fence and headed toward the finish line, I flung my fist into the air in a salute to Helios and Demeter, to Pegasus and the Navajo spirits, to all the gods of horse and flight. Our first challenge had gone well. Our relationship had stood the test of stress and speed; we had shown ourselves to be a team.

I couldn't wait to do it all again—and do it again—and again—we did.

Behold
My sovereign Lady
Crisp the guinea ground

Spendthrift branches
Scatter gold on gold

Paddock-bound
Under awnings riven
We (medallion pair
Sunstruck this Moulton morning)
Light-encircled seem
Alchemically given
One sole self to share

A centaur's dream
I know

Meanwhile
The gate hangs wide
With Jack beside

"Just see her go!"

We smile

O, now she is herself
Mine no more than flashing water
Dissolved in radiant air
Already in a wild half-circle
Gone plunging fifty yards,
Head twisted down, towards her own truth

Her tail plumes
Her hoofs glitter

Unbridled, charged by joyous scorn
Spirit-swelled, she kicks away
Box,
Tack
School
Grooms
All our wickedness
All mishandlings since she was born

And I, forsworn
Find her
Lost to my mange
Lovely beyond telling
Transformed
Cresting some brilliant wave
That she alone can see
Up reaching

Mounted on some capricious cloud
Pegasus should serve
This divinity

Peter Cornish, from *"Lady Midas"*

AUTHOR BARBARA WILDER writes, "What I call freedom is the ability to live the life we came to live and express to the fullest who we truly are. To experience freedom, we must give up control and instead become more and more conscious of the subtle messages, the rhythms, and the signs that are constantly around us to guide us toward our freedom." By their very nature, horses make us readers of subtle message and rhythm, of invisible sign. They show us what an unconditional relationship means. They give us perspective on nature and everyday life. They provide us with insights into how to make decisions and solve problems. Horses connect us to our most intimate feelings of delight and pleasure and satisfy our need to nurture and to be nurtured. They give us love and accept our love. Horses help us find our fullest and truest accepting selves, which, after all, is where freedom begins.

For years I had handled my father's horses, fed them, ridden them, groomed them, and loved them. But I had never owned one.

Now I owned one. . . . The colt was to be mine, and no one could ever touch him, or ride him, or feed him, or nurse him—no one except myself. . . .

I remember that when the foaling box was cleaned, the light turned down again, and Otieno left to watch over the newly born, I went out and walked with Buller beyond the stables and a little way down the path that used to lead to Arab Maina's.

I thought about the new colt, Otieno's Promised Land, how big the world must be, and then about the colt again. What shall I name him?

Who doesn't look upward when searching for a name?

*Looking upward, what is there but the sky to see? And
seeing it, how can the name or the hope be earthbound?
Was there a horse named Pegasus that flew? Was there a
horse with wings?*

*Yes, once there was—once, long ago, there was. And
now there is again.*

Beryl Markham, *West With the Night*

THE LADY OF the seventeenth century rode sidesaddle,
both legs draped over one side of the horse, her body
struggling to maintain balance. Her saddle offered no
horn to hold. She rode in a full skirt, with petticoats, a
tight waistcoat, a ruffled blouse, gloves, and a beribboned
hat. Toppling to the ground was not just a fear but a prob-
ability, and remounting in the field a considerable challenge. If she was in the "increasing way," as she often was,
her pregnancy multiplied the risk. Danger was imminent,
and yet she rode.

The lady rode despite the risks because it was in her to
ride and because riding addressed her deepest yearnings.
Riding swept her beyond the walls of the manor and into a
greater natural world where she was free of all but the
rhythm of the horse's hooves on the earth. Riding carved a
time of self-indulgence into her day and gave her an unconditionally loving friend with whom to spend it—her
horse. On the back of her mount, she could rise above her
own height, race beyond her own speed, see from other
than her own eyes, leave behind her worldly cares. Alone
with her horse, she could listen to her heart and connect
with her soul and take her own measure. When she dis-
mounted at the stable, she carried the power of the ride
back into her home.

Women have always ridden to be free. They doffed their skirts and straddled horses to ride into the Crusades. They masqueraded as men to explore and tame the Old West. They were frontier nurse Mary Breckinridge in eastern Kentucky, Elisabeth the Empress of Austria, outlaw Belle Starr, performer Annie Oakley, seventeenth-century travel writer Celia Fiennes, and adventurer Isabella Bird. On horseback, they led invading armies—or escaped them. With horses, they broke ground and broke tradition.

Women have been riding horses into myth and fable and imagination as long as women have sought to be free. When I greet my horse, when I stroke her warm coat, when I lift myself onto her back, I join not her alone but all the women and all the horses who have run wild together since the dawn of memory, and I am made whole.

As doth an Egle,
whan him list to sore,
This same stede whall bere you evirmore,
Withoutin harme,
till you ben there you lest,
Though that you slepin on his bak and rest.

> Geoffrey Chaucer, English poet
> "The Squire's Tale," *Canterbury Tales*

OUR LAST HORSE trial of the season was in Jackson, Wyoming. This is a high-level international competition with hundreds of horses from the western United States competing. Theo performed well in the dressage phase and moved beautifully over the cross-country course despite one brief disagreement at the water complex. Even so, during the show-jumping phase on the fourth and final day of the competition, she expressed a strong opinion about her readiness to go home. She had had enough of living in a box with no free horse time for five days. She wanted to head back to her comfortable Colorado home. Freedom for Theo's body, as for all women's bodies, requires freedom for her spirit, and her spirit was developing a cramp.

On that final day, she was jumping well but was clearly distracted. She started backing up when I asked her to go near the gate to the competition ring. After circling her several times, we managed to gallop into the ring and stop to salute the judges. She completed the jumping course with no faults but in a rapid, let's-get-this-over-with manner. I knew she had given a great effort but could give no more. We finished a respectable fifth in the competition, and I was proud of her. One sign of a healthy intimate relationship is the freedom to express ourselves. Theo and I had grown so close that she was free to say *Mary, let's go home*. And we did.

EMPRESS ELISABETH OF AUSTRIA,
CIRCUS RIDER

*Her titles were Empress Elisabeth of Austria and
Queen Elisabeth of Hungary. To adoring Hungarian subjects she was "Sisi," but the haughty Viennese bourgeoisie
were not so approving. They called her "Circus Rider."*

*The Empress Elisabeth was born in 1837 to the
Bavarian Duke Maximilian Joseph, an avid rider and
huntsman who became a model for the high-spirited
young girl. A great natural beauty, Elisabeth made it
clear from an early age that she preferred the blood sports
and open country riding of her father to sitting with
guests at the castle. It was sometimes said the free-
spirited young aristocrat preferred horses to people, and
one modern-day biographer has written, "The way to her
heart was known to be through the hoof."*

*After marrying Franz Joseph, Emperor of Austria, she
rarely held court but often rode out with the hunt. When
her eldest daughter died in childhood, she turned to the
stables for consolation. At the imperial riding school and
in the public parks, she could be found exercising morning and afternoon, sometimes three or four different
horses in sequence for as many as seven hours a day. The
empress often rode bareback and took to performing
stunts such as standing and kneeling on her galloping
horses. She became proficient at* haute école—*an equestrian art sometimes referred to as "airs above the
ground"—and she spent endless hours training with the*

*Spanish Riding School masters. Her instructor in Vienna
said, "She has the knack of pulling herself into immediate and almost mesmeric communication with her horse."
Her favorite horse was Bravo, a gelding, who "flew and
was full of fire."*

*Her love of horses and riding colored virtually every
facet of the empress's life. She rode even when newly delivered of a baby, and she consistently brushed aside con-
ventions that kept most European highborn women in
corsets and crinolines. When she visited England and Ireland with the express purpose of riding with their notoriously reckless and wild hunts, she sought out a famed
Scottish horseman, William George "Bay" Middleton, to
lead her in the ride to the hounds. Her equestrian feats in
the British Isles won Middleton's praise and drew crowds
who raised triumphal arches on the roads she traveled before returning home.*

*The monarch's lack of convention came at a price. Al-
though popular with her subjects, she offended Viennese
high society with her disregard for the rigid etiquette of
the day. The oversight of her children was taken forcibly
from her and given to her mother-in-law at the Viennese
court. An "empress against her will," Elisabeth escaped
the confines of royal life by traveling, especially to Hungary, where she could "gallop to exhaustion" on her
30,000-acre estate, Gödöllo. She kept twenty-six hunters
on the grounds for her rides to the hunt there, operated a
riding school, and learned to be a trainer herself.*

*Elisabeth's horses carried her to a freedom almost un-
heard of in her day. They helped her set a bold example*

of fitness and athleticism, they comforted her, they dazzled others, and they brought her acclaim to offset scorn. No matter what the court in Vienna might whisper about her, Elisabeth always found equine friends in the stable and the field.

Elisabeth, Empress of Austria was assassinated by an Italian anarchist in 1898 at the age of sixty. She was widely mourned by the people of Hungary, whose autonomy within the Austro-Hungarian Empire she had been instrumental in securing, and she remains respected and loved there to this day. Once considered the most beautiful monarch in Europe, the "Circus Rider" is frequently pictured seated on one of her steeds.

"She could be no feminist, given her birth and circumstances," writes Andrew Sinclair in his biography Death by Fame: A Life of Elisabeth, Empress of Austria. *"Yet she could set an example by her daring and her ways."*

> *"The bright star of Europe" her kingdom has left,*
> *And Austria mourns of its Empress bereft.*
> *Firm seat in the saddle: light hands on the reins,*
> *As e'er guided steed over Hungary's plains:*
> *She has come with her beauty, grace, courage*
>   *and skill*
> *To ride, with our hounds, from old Shuckburgh*
>   *Hill.*

Unknown balladeer
contemporary with the empress
Also taken from *Death by Fame*

AFTERWORD

She Flies Without Wings is a book that found an unexpected beginning in a program I created many years ago for horsewomen. A rider nearly all my life, I had discovered that the horse-handling and riding techniques that worked for men didn't necessarily work for women. My program, Women & Horses™, offered a fitness and performance system designed specifically for the female equestrian.

After several years of producing and presenting workshops on the program, I wrote a resource and exercise guide called *Fitness, Performance and the Female Equestrian* (Macmillan). *Fitness* is still going strong, and I continue to speak about rider fitness, but as I met horsewomen around the country and the world, I was continually reminded that there is more to the relationship of women and horses than physical enjoyment and good health. Over the years I noticed that when women talked about horses, their faces took on a special light. Their eyes sparkled, they laughed easily, and any natural reserve they felt about talking to a stranger about deeply personal feelings evaporated. These reactions weren't limited to horsewomen. I also met women who rarely rode or who never did, women who had only fantasized about knowing or owning a horse, women who had ridden as children but not since; when the topic was horses, the same light illuminated them all. Horses had always brought a great deal more into my life than mere physical fitness and pleasure, but, as I talked with large numbers of other women, I realized that the connection I felt with the horse was a connection many women felt. *Someday*, I thought, *I will write about this bond*.

It was when I moved to Colorado a few years ago that this *someday* arrived. With the abundance of blue skies and dry air in the Rocky Mountains, it is hard to be out of doors and not be touched and moved. Ranging the countryside with my horse Theo, I was struck time and again by the spiritual gifts that came when she and I were keeping company. *We don't have to work at this,* I thought. *The landscape may be new and different but every step my horse and I share is natural and familiar.* It was as if, when we stepped from the barn together, we passed into a refreshing and sacred world.

It is this sacred world and the juncture where it meets and enriches our everyday lives that *She Flies Without Wings* explores.

ACKNOWLEDGMENTS

Thank you to my husband, best friend, and life partner, Tom Aronson. His deep sense of love, thoughtfulness, and compassion for our life together continues to amaze and inspire me.

I am forever grateful to the author and horsewoman Evelyn Kaye whom I met through my horse business when I first arrived in Boulder. She invited me to join the Boulder Media Women's group and meet with them on Friday mornings for coffee. I was instantly fascinated by the diversity of the women I was meeting and the talent contained within this group. What a joy and a resource this group came to mean to my career and my life. During one of our monthly potluck dinners I met another special professional in the literary trade named Jody Rein. We spent a great deal of time talking about her career in publishing and my dreams with my Women & Horses™ program. Over a glass of red wine we gained enthusiasm as we discussed ideas for my next book. Jody and I met again during lunch and decided to undertake the book project together. Jody became my literary representative. What a thrill this was and is for me to get this long-awaited project under way with an exceptionally skilled professional to give me direction.

Thank you to a very special editor at Delacorte Press, Danielle Perez. She has been supportive and enthusiastic from beginning to end.

Thank you to Doris Sanger Fuller, for being an outstanding editor, wordsmith, and supportive friend through the countless hours this project required. Thank you to Lisa DeYoung for assistance with permissions and attributions.

Thank you to my horse angels who have enriched my life, women's lives, and the lives of numerous horses: Peggy Cummings, Margaret Watters, and Helen Junkin. Thank you to my grandfather Dan B. Midkiff Sr. who gave me the horse gene and the sparkle in my eyes when I see a beautiful horse. Thank you to my father, Dan B. Midkiff Jr., for establishing a solid foundation for me to become a hard worker and a responsible caring human being, and to my mother, Jane Midkiff Polk, for her love and for setting an example for me and many others to follow in the search for spiritual health, adventure, and feminine strength.

Thank you to my stepfather, Reed Polk, for his ever-present positive support and love. Thank you to my brother, Dan B. Midkiff III, and his wife, Su, for their enthusiasm over this project. And to my stepmother, Pattie Midkiff, thank you for sweet inspiration.

Thank you to the members of the Boulder Media Women's group, especially Pattie Logan, Jana Kuchtova, and Barbara Wilder, for providing me with resources for research and creativity.

Thank you to my horsy friends and borders at the Foothills Equestrian Center, where Theo lives. Thank you to friends, instructors, and trainers Tom Betts, Jennifer and Philip Oldham, and Marty Marten for supporting Theo and me through our competitions. Thank you to Manuel Garcia, Ismael Garcia, and Carol Walker for taking exceptionally good care of Theo when I could not be there. Thank you to Theo's team of healthcare professionals, Dr. Nancy Loving, Dr. Rachel Blackmer, Dr. Ed Boldt, Jim Pascucci, John James, and Dr. Michael Pavsek. And my healthcare providers Dr. Doug Kennedy, everyone at Penrose Healing Arts, Helios Health Center, and Dr. Larry Eckstein.

Thank you to the authors, ancient or contemporary, who provided the beautiful and meaningful passages, poetry, and rhyme featured within this work and for honoring the horse in all of her glory. Thank you to the women I interviewed and those who contributed material for the book: Grambs Aronson, Madelyn Sullivan, Joyce Nesmith, C. J. McKague, Missy Hollingsworth, Moe Wilson, and Tina Beckley. Thank you to all of the women (and men) who attended my Women & Horses™ programs over the years and helped make this project possible.

For providing unlimited resources, thank you to the Naropa Institute, National Sporting Library, Colonial Williamsburg Foundation, Cowgirl Hall of Fame, Denver Public Library, University of Colorado's Norlin Library, Boulder Public Library, J.A. Allen Book Publishers, and numerous bookstores in England and the United States.

Thank you to Theodora, Diva, Tory, Bandit, Baron, Ginger, Blue, Belle Breezin', Handaul, Midnight, Sam, Sergeant, Iolanthe, Festival, Queen's Village, Lofty, Harmonica, Weeong, and the many countless horses I have worked with, admired, and loved over my lifetime. Also an apology to those horses that I was too strong with or didn't understand; thank you for tolerating my ignorance.

Thank you to our dog, Boomer, who is always at my side.

BIBLIOGRAPHY

Andrews, Lynn. *Windhorse Woman: A Marriage of Spirit.* New York: Warner Books, 1989.

Austen, Jane. *Mansfield Park.* New York: Barnes & Noble Books, 1999.

Bagnold, Enid. *National Velvet.* New York: William Morrow & Co., 1935.

Bauer, C. A. *The White Horses.* New York: Kensington Publishing Corp., 1999.

Benjamin Park. "Alexander Taming Bucephalus." In *Songs of Horses,* ed. Robert Frothingham. Cambridge, MA: Houghton Mifflin, 1920.

Bird, Isabella. *A Lady's Life in the Rocky Mountains.* Norman: University of Oklahoma Press, 1960.

———. *Six Months in the Sandwich Islands.* Honolulu: University of Hawaii Press, 1964.

Boucher, Susan. "Partnering Pegasus." In *Intimate Nature: The Bond Between Women and Animals,* ed. Linda Hogan et al. New York: Fawcett Books/The Ballantine Publishing Group, 1998.

Brackenbury, Alison. "Breaking Out." In *The Poetry of Horses,* ed. Olwen Way. London: J. A. Allen, 1994.

Burlin, Natalie Curtis. *The Indians' Book.* New York: Harper & Bros., 1907.

Buyer, Laurie Wagner. "Growing Tomatoes." In *Glass-Eyed Paint in the Rain.* Glendo, WY: High Plains Press, 1996.

Campbell, Joseph. *The Power of Myth.* New York: Doubleday, 1988.

Caras, Roger. *A Perfect Harmony: The Intertwining Lives of Animals and Humans.* New York: Simon & Schuster, 1996.

Clark, LaVerne Harrell. *They Sang for Horses.* Tucson: University of Arizona Press, 1966.

Clutton-Brock, Juliet. *Horse Power.* Cambridge, MA: Harvard University Press, 1992.

Coolidge, Dave, and Mary Robeas Coolidge. *The Navajo Indians.* Boston: Houghton Mifflin, 1930.

Cooper, J. C., editor. *An Illustrated Encyclopedia of Traditional Symbols.* London: Thames and Hudson, 1978.

Cornish, Peter. "Lady Midas." In *The Poetry of Horses,* ed. Olwen Way. London: J. A. Allen, 1994.

Cronin, Patricia. "Pony Tales." In *Horse People, Writers and Artists on the Horses They Love,* ed. Michael J. Rosen. New York: Workman Publishing Co., 1998.

Dent, Anthony. *Horses in Shakespeare's England.* London: J. A. Allen, 1987.

Dickens, Monica. *Talking of Horses*. London: William Heinemann, 1973.

Dimmick, Barbara. *In the Presence of Horses: A Novel*. New York: Bantam/Doubleday, 1998.

Dobie, J. Frank. "The White Steed of the Prairies." In *Tales of the Mustang*. Dallas: The Book Club of Texas, 1936.

Dossenbach, Monique, and Hans Dossenbach, ed. *The Noble Horse*. New York: Portland House, 1987.

Eardley, Carla Jean. "The Woman Who Was Part Horse." In *Southwestern Women: New Voices*, ed. Caitlin L. Gannon. Tucson: Javelina Press, 1997.

Ehrlich, Gretel. "The Solace of Open Spaces." In *Intimate Nature: The Bond Between Women and Animals*, ed. Linda Hogan et al. New York: Fawcett Books/The Ballantine Publishing Group, 1998.

Eisenkraft-Palazzola, Lori. *Faeries: A Doorway to the Enchanted Realm*. New York: Smithmark Publishers, 1999.

Estés, Clarissa Pinkola. *Women Who Run with the Wolves*. New York: Ballantine Books, 1992.

Evans, Ivor H., ed. *Brewer's Dictionary of Phrase and Fable*, 15th ed. New York: Harper & Row, 1817.

Exley, Helen, ed. *Horses: The Best Quotes and Most Glorious Paintings*. New York: Exley Giftbooks, 1994.

Fiennes, Celia. *The Illustrated Journal of Celia Fiennes 1662–1741*. London: Cresset Press, 1947.

Findlay, Patricia. *Parsifal Perhaps: A Classical Courtship*. Chippenham, UK: The Self Publishing Assn./Antony Rowe, 1988.

The Folk-Lore Record, vol. 2. London: Nichols & Sons, 1879.

Francisco, Nia. "Escaping the Turquoise Sky." In *Blue Horses for Navajo Women*. Greenfield Center, NY: Greenfield Review Press, 1988.

Frothingham, Robert, ed. *Songs of Horses*. Cambridge, MA: Houghton Mifflin, 1920.

Fry, Christopher. "Venus Observed." In *The Poetry of Horses*, ed. Olwen Way. London: J. A. Allen, 1994.

Fuller, Margaret. "Woman in the Nineteenth Century (1845)." In *Literature by Women*, ed. Sandra M. Gilbert. New York: W. W. Norton, 1996.

Glancy, Diane. "Lead Horse." In *Earth Song, Sky Spirit: Short Stories of the Contemporary Native American Experience*, ed. Clifford E. Trafzer. New York: Anchor Books/Doubleday, 1993.

Goble, Paul. *The Gift of the Sacred Dog*. Scarsdale, NY: Bradbury Press, 1980.

Griffin, Susan. *Woman & Nature: The Roaring Inside Her*. New York: Harper Colophon Books/Harper & Row, 1978.

Griffiths, Helen. *Horse in the Clouds.* London: Hutchinson & Co., 1957.

Guiney, Louise Imogen. "The Wild Ride." In *Modern American Poetry: An Introduction,* ed. Louis Untermeyer. New York: Harcourt, Brace & Howe, 1919.

Harjo, Joy. "Interview." *Kalliope: A Journal of Women's Art,* 13, no. 2 (1983).

Harman, Samuel W. *Hell on the Border.* Houston: Frontier Press of Texas, 1954.

Hays, Helen Ireland. "Horse Tales." *New York Folklore Quarterly,* 20, no. 4 (Dec. 1964).

Heath, Jennifer. *On the Edge of Dream.* New York: Penguin Putnam, 1998.

Helprin, Mark. *Winter's Tale.* New York: Harcourt Brace Jovanovich, 1983.

Henry, Marguerite. *Sea Star, Orphan of Chincoteague.* New York: Simon & Schuster, 1949.

Herriott, James. *It Shouldn't Happen to a Vet.* London: Michael Joseph Ltd., 1970.

Hogan, Linda. *Red Clay: Poems and Stories.* Greenfield Center, NY: Greenfield Review Press, 1991.

Howey, M. Oldfield, ed. *The Horse in Magic and Myth.* London: William Ryder & Sons, 1923.

Hughes, Ted. "Phaethon." In *Tales from Ovid.* New York: Farrar Straus & Giroux, 1997.

Ivy, Robin. "Child Rider." In *The Poetry of Horses,* ed. Olwen Way. London: J. A. Allen, 1994.

Jobes, Gertrude, ed. *Dictionary of Mythology, Folklore and Symbols.* Part I. New York: Scarecrow Press, 1962.

Knowles, James Sheridan. *The Love Chase: A Comedy, in Five Acts.* London: E. Moxon, 1837, Act II, scene iii.

LeGuin, Ursula K. *A Ride on the Red Mare's Back.* New York: Orchard Books, 1992.

Llewelyn, Morgan. *The Horse Goddess.* New York: Tom Doherty Associates, 1982.

Maharam, Trish. "Elegy for Diamond." In *Intimate Nature: The Bond Between Women and Animals,* ed. Linda Hogan et al. New York: Fawcett Books/The Ballantine Publishing Group, 1998.

Mapson, Jo-Ann. *Hank & Chloe.* New York: Harper Trade, 1994.

Markham, Beryl. *West With the Night.* New York: North Point Press/Farrar Straus & Giroux, 1983.

McCarriston, Linda. "Healing the Mare." In *Intimate Nature: The Bond Between Women and Animals,* ed. Linda Hogan et al. New York: Fawcett Books/The Ballantine Publishing Group, 1998.

McCormick, Adele, and Marlena McCormick. *Horse Sense & The Human Heart.* Deerfield Beach, FL: Health Communications, 1997.

Niedecker, Lorine. "Horse, Hello." In *T & G: Collected Poems (1936–1966).* New York: Small Publishers' Co., 1968.

Perkins, Charles Elliot. *The Pinto Horse.* Santa Barbara, CA: Wallace Hebberd, 1927.

———. *The Pinto Horse and the Phantom Bull.* Lincoln: University of Nebraska Press, 1998.

Petroski, Catherine. "Beautiful My Mane in the Wind." In *Gravity and Other Stories.* Boston: Faber and Faber, 1981.

Price, Steven D., ed. *The Quotable Horse Lover.* New York: The Lyons Press, 1999.

Ruepp, Krista. *Midnight Rider.* New York: North-South Books, 1995.

Sandburg, Helga. *Blueberry.* New York: Dial Books for Young Readers, 1963.

Seth-Smith, Michael, ed. *The Horse in Art and History.* London: New English Library, 1978.

Shirley, Glenn. *Belle Starr and Her Times.* Norman: University of Oklahoma Press, 1982.

Sinclair, Andrew. *Death by Fame.* New York: St. Martin's Press, 1998.

Smith, Betty. *A Tree Grows in Brooklyn.* New York: HarperTrade, 1998.

Sneyd, Barbara. *Riding High.* New York: Dodd, Mead and Co., 1986.

Stace, Marjorie. "Racing Rivals." In *Horse and Pony Stories for Girls.* London: Hamlyn Publishing Group, 1971.

Tapahonso, Luci. *Blue Horses Rush In.* Tucson: University of Arizona Press, 1996.

Untermeyer, Louis. "The Horse of Sienna." In *The Donkey of God and Other Stories.* New York: Golden Press, 1954.

Van der Post, Laurens. *About Blady: A Pattern Out of Time.* New York: William Morrow, 1991.

Vincenz, Stanislaw. *On the High Uplands: Sagas, Songs, Tales and Legends of the Carpathians,* trans. H. C. Stevens. New York: Roy Publishers, 1955.

Walker, Barbara G., ed. *The Woman's Encyclopedia of Myths and Secrets.* New York: HarperCollins, 1983.

Way, Olwen. *The Poetry of Horses.* London: J. A. Allen, 1994.

Welcome, John. *The Sporting Empress.* London: Michael Joseph, 1975.

Wolfe, Tom. *A Man in Full.* New York: Farrar Straus & Giroux, 1999.

Zabolotsky, Nikolai Alekseevich. "The Face of the Horse." In *The Poetry of Horses,* ed. Olwen Way. London: J. A. Allen, 1994.

PERMISSIONS

ABOUT THE AUTHOR

MARY D. MIDKIFF is the creator of Women and Horses™, a fitness and performance program specific to the female equestrian. She has been conducting presentations and clinics around the world for the past ten years. She is also the president of Equestrian Resources, a marketing firm specializing in the promotion of show, sport, and recreational horse activities. She is the author of *Fitness, Performance, and the Female Equestrian,* and lives in Boulder, Colorado.